# CAPITAL FORMATION IN SOUTH-WEST ENGLAND



Edited by

Walter Minchinton

Professor of Economic History

University of Exeter

University of Exeter

1978

ISBN 0 85989 038 4

CONTENTS

# INTRODUCTION

One of the aspects of British economic history to which a great deal of attention has been directed recently is that of capital formation.[1] The early historians of British industrial development, as François Crouzet has pointed out, did not pay much attention to the question of capital formation; they were far more interested in the institutional, technical and social aspects of the industrial revolution than in its economic problems. Their approach was descriptive rather than analytical and lacked any theoretical framework. They concentrated on the rise of the factory system, of industrial capitalism and on the 'hegemony' which capital established over industry.[2] But since 1945 there have been a number of attempts to assess how much capital was required, the types of capital (whether fixed or circulating) needed, the methods of accumulation and the variations in ownership. In this volume are printed three papers which were given at a research seminar held at the Devon Centre for Further Education, Dartington on 29-30 January 1977, where the discussions benefited particularly from the contributions of Charles Feinstein, John Parry-Lewis and William Reader, together with a subsequent re-working of material on the Exeter housing market, presented at the seminar by John Parry-Lewis.

Capital formation has been defined as 'the additions made during a particular period of time to the stock of goods which are for use in future production. These are both fixed assets, such as buildings, items of plant and so on, and work in progress, stocks of raw materials and finished goods. A distinction is usually made between gross fixed capital formation - that is, the addition of new fixed assets to the stock during the period - and net fixed capital formation which takes into account allowances for depreciation of the existing stock of fixed assets'.[3] In his paper at the seminar, whose purpose was to set the scene and establish the nature of the issues involved, Jeffrey Coates argued that capital formation provided not only plant, machinery and working capital for the production of goods but also for the generation of a flow of services. This process of investment, it was suggested in the discussion, was influenced by a number of factors of which the most important was technological change with innovations in production techniques of greater importance than innovation in marketing.

This exposition was followed by papers on two of the basic industries of the west country, woollen textiles and metal mining. In both of these the main theme was the shift from labour-intensive to capital-intensive methods of production. Because of the relative simplicity and cheapness of machinery in the early stages of industrialisation, working capital was of considerable importance in the west of England woollen textile industry. Such limited capital requirements could be largely met by the clothiers and their families. This account therefore provides a companion study to

1 See, in particular, James P P Higgins and Sidney Pollard, *Aspects of capital investment in Great Britain, 1750-1850: a preliminary survey* (Methuen, 1971); François Crouzet, ed. *Capital formation in the industrial revolution* (Methuen, 1972); Brian L Anderson, ed. *Capital accumulation in the industrial revolution* (Dent, 1974); and Charles Feinstein, 'Capital accumulation and economic growth in Great Britain, 1760-1860' in *Cambridge economic history of Europe, VII.*

2 Crouzet, ed. *Capital formation,* p.2 and p.2 note 1.

3 John Hibbert, 'Modern practices and conventions in measuring capital formation in the national accounts' in Higgins and Pollard, *Aspects of capital investment,* p.11.

Herbert Heaton's discussion of the finance of the Yorkshire textile industry in which he made a number of points: that little capital needed to be sunk in buildings and equipment or in raw materials and that since both the raw material market and the method of selling cloth had for centuries been organised to cater for the small producer, a small factory with few machines was not at a great disadvantage in competing with a larger rival. Further, external supplies of capital were less important than the personal or family sources of funds.[1] And, as the business continued, the source of finance was largely personal. Partners in the Wiltshire woollen firms did not pay themselves a salary but drew out an agreed amount each year depending on the state of trade. But new techniques adopted in the course of the nineteenth century required more to be spent on machinery and so the industry became more capital-intensive. In his discussion of events, Kenneth Ponting drew on local newspapers, church records and rate returns, because of the relative sparsity of business records, to concentrate on the changing fortunes of individual businesses. He noted that the firms which were successful were innovators in new types of cloth rather than in new methods of manufacture. And in a personal statement in the discussion which took him beyond the time limits of his paper, Kenneth Ponting stated that the profit return of his firm in the 1930s as a result of their move into the ladies' dress trade was 20 per cent compared with about 5 per cent for the woollen industry as a whole. Later, we were, he said, the first firm in the Trowbridge area to mix synthetic fibre and wool which produced a cheaper fabric to compete with the then fashionable grey flannel. This session therefore provided not only a useful account of one aspect of the Wiltshire woollen industry from the later eighteenth century but some insight into the twentieth-century problems of the industry.

Provided the accounts are kept with reasonable care and are available to him, the historian has a relatively simple task in attempting to estimate capital formation in a manufacturing industry like the west of England woollen textile industry. Much greater difficulty of necessity is encountered in performing a similar operation with respect to mining. In order to make some assessment of the position in the west of England metal mining industry, Christopher Schmitz has based his calculations on work already done which relates not to mining in Britain but to mining in the United States. Using American capital-output ratios which, tentative in themselves, inevitably reflect the different situation there, Schmitz has produced some estimates for metal mining in south-west England. In so doing he provides not only a vivid illustration of the problems involved in translating these concepts into practice but also a useful account of the techniques employed in metal mining, particularly of the problems faced in sinking shafts in search of increasingly inaccessible ores. Together with the introduction of the steam engine, such investment made metal-mining much more capital-intensive. Compared with manufacturing industry, in which there are normally two elements - capital formation and depreciation - mining requires a third component which can be defined as scrapping and consists of the taking out of capital stock whether by the closure of old shafts or the unproductive construction of shafts and levels.

Finally, a note on the Exeter housing market draws on information collected by the late Bernard Weber to underline the important role played

1 'Financing the industrial revolution' in Crouzet, ed. *Capital formation,* pp.85-9.

by building and construction in total capital formation. In so doing, it enables a comparison to be made between the cyclical fluctuations in housing construction in a provincial city and the behaviour of this volatile sector nationally. A statistical analysis of the inter-war figures[1] shows that there was a close relationship between the number of houses built annually in Exeter and nationally and, as might be expected, a weaker relationship between the number of plans deposited in Exeter each year and the number of houses built in Great Britain.[2] Unfortunately, for the period 1867-1914 the figures are not available for the number of houses built in Exeter each year and so a comparison can only be made between Exeter plans and Great Britain houses. Even so, there is still a statistically significant relationship between the number of plans deposited in Exeter each year and the number of houses built nationally.[3] An analogy with the inter-war period suggests that if figures of houses built in Exeter in this period were available, the relationship between the number of Exeter houses and the number of Great Britain houses built between 1867 and 1914 would have been statistically significant. It therefore serves to cast doubt on the statement made below, that table 2 shows that 'Exeter builders went their own way without too much regard for national trends' until the end of the nineteenth century.[4]

Incidentally this paper illustrates the problems which arise from the nature of the information available for analysis: plans deposited or houses completed.[5] But the task of comparing the position with regard to house building in the period 1867-1940 was rendered easier by the fact that there were no substantial technological changes in the construction industry during this time.

Other issues raised in discussion concerned the nature of the local capital markets in the south-west of England and the extent to which they were able to operate independently of London. The improvement in transport facilities such as the construction of the turnpikes was one factor helping

1 See tables 1 and 4, pp. 56 and 59 below.

2 Writing GB houses as X, Exeter houses as Y and Exeter plans as Z, then the least squares regressions of Y and Z on X, fitted to data relating to 1920-40, are, respectively (estimated standard errors in parentheses):
$Y = -20.8642 + 1.0910X$, $r = +0.9350$ (significant at 1/1000 level)
(22.4941) (0.0949) DW = 0.97
and
$Z = -3.8005 + 1.4305X$, $r = +0.8136$ (significant at 1/1000 level)
(55.5867) (0.2342) DW = 1.29
I am indebted to my colleague, Dr Frank Oliver, for these calculations and those in footnote 3 below.

3 The figures are given in table 2, p. 57 below. Using the same notation as in footnote 2 above, the regression of Z on X fitted to the data relating to 1867-1914 is:
$Z = -27.8491 + 1.6778X$, $r = +0.4343$ (significant at 1/1000 level)
(52.2994) (0.5131) DW = 0.75

4 See below, p. 56.

5 A fuller discussion of this subject would take note of the figures provided by Robert Newton, *Victorian Exeter* (Leicester UP, 1968) p. 304.

to create a national capital market.[1] One consequence of the growing integration of local economies into a national economy in the early nineteenth century was that the movement of local interest rates came to be more closely correlated with the changes in the London market. A further theme explored was the development of appropriate institutional forms as the needs for capital changed and expanded. The importance of the attorney in rural areas in particular was stressed.[2]

Limited in scope by the restraints of a twenty-four hour conference, these papers and the related discussion serve nonetheless to extend our knowledge of capital formation in Britain since the middle of the eighteenth century by a consideration of particular problems facing business men in the south-west of England. But they by no means exhaust the discussion. Other aspects of capital formation merit consideration, other industries - extractive, manufacturing and service - deserve consideration as do the institutions available for the mobilisation of capital which operated within a legal framework. The significance of political and social factors in influencing both the volume and direction of investment also merit examination. And, a severer task, it would not be without interest to attempt a disaggregation of the national figures to see if it were possible to produce a set of figures for capital formation in the south-west as a region.

Walter Minchinton

1 It is hoped to publish this paper in a forthcoming volume.

2 See Brian L Anderson, 'The attorney and the early capital market in Lancashire' in Crouzet, ed. *Capital formation*, pp.223-55.

# CAPITAL FORMATION - AN ECONOMIST'S VIEW

Jeffrey H Coates

The process of capital formation is central to an understanding of the causes of economic growth and development and also of the cyclical nature of economic activity. Thus it is not surprising, given the magnitude of such problems as the dire poverty in which so many millions subsist in the third world and the periodic bouts of unemployment characterising the industrialised nations, that economists have devoted so much attention to it. It would be wrong to suggest, however, that the importance of capital formation cannot be overstated. Indeed there are at least two notable examples where the role of capital formation as such has been overstated, both of which being rooted in the same mistaken assumption about the significance of the *level* of capital formation. The first is the belief that, by achieving a certain magic proportion of national resources devoted to capital formation, self-sustaining economic growth would follow more or less as a matter of course. This seems to be the result of trying to apply as a general rule, the particular experience of the industrial revolution in Britain. The notion is all the more suspect, given that substantial controversy has arisen over the increases in the ratio of savings and investment actually achieved during the period. The second example concerns international comparisons of growth performance. There is a widely-held belief that the relatively slow rate of growth of countries such as the UK and the USA in recent years is the result of the observed tendencies of those countries to devote a lower proportion of their gross national product to fixed capital formation than their more successful competitors. But the *composition* of investment expenditures may be more significant, in fact, than their level; it could be argued that too much emphasis has been placed on prestige projects (Concorde and space exploration) at the expense of commercial projects.

But, if the achievement of a higher level of capital formation may not of itself guarantee economic growth, it is certainly an essential ingredient, not only because investment expenditure leads, via the multiplier process, to higher incomes but also because it increases productive potential in two basic ways. Firstly, a larger stock of capital facilitates the production of more goods and services with a given level of technology. Secondly, capital formation is of major and probably increasing significance as the vehicle by which the benefits of technical progress are realised and technical advances are 'embodied' in capital equipment.

Any historical treatment of the determinants of capital formation and hence of economic progress must also consider the importance of technological innovation as a fundamental driving force. Although economists have taken note of technical change in their growth models, there has not (with the important exception of Schumpeter) been much attempt until fairly recently to develop a rigorous and systematic treatment of the processes of invention, innovation and technological diffusion. Perhaps the explanation lies in an apparent obsession with the readily *quantifiable* aspects of growth to the exclusion of more *qualitative* (but not necessarily less significant) factors.

The process of capital formation and economic progress has been one of successive exploitation of new advances in techniques and especially new products, new materials and new forms of transport, which have generated huge waves of investment spending and possibly also very long-term business cycles (Kondratieff cycles). Examples spring readily to mind: the railway, steel, electrification, the motor car, radio and television, and synthetic fibres. Each of these developments induced investment in associated industries which in turn, through the operation of the multiplier, generated high levels of income and consumption. Economic progress still depends, and possibly to a larger extent than ever, on technological innovation but more recently the process has been less one of developing really significant single advances of the kind outlined in the examples above. Now the process is more widespread and systematic and derives increasingly from a deliberate commitment of resources to research and development by the corporate sector and also by the state.

In the post-war period innovation has been largely consumer-oriented with consumer durables leading the spectacular increase in living standards in many industrialised countries. But there have also been continuous advances in, for instance, chemicals, pharmaceuticals and electronic capital goods and it is significant that the most dynamic sectors in industry and international trade are science-based.

## Some fundamental definitions and distinctions

By capital is meant a collection of man-made resources which, in conjunction with labour, produces a flow of goods and services or income. In this context the concern is with real capital (in the form of tangible assets) as distinct from financial capital. The importance of changes in the nature and variety of financial claims to capital formation will be taken up later. The distinction between money flows and a real adjustment of productive capacity is significant in the context of the Keynesian equilibrium requirement for equality between saving and investment or in the warranted rate of growth of Harrod-Domar models. Such equality in the real sense is obviously conditioned by supply elasticities in capital goods industries. Real capital may be further sub-divided into fixed capital and working capital, the latter comprising, *inter alia*, stocks of raw materials, work in progress and inventories of finished goods. Hence real gross capital formation includes the process of adding to the stock of capital goods, buildings, producers' durables, net changes in inventories and (in an open economy) net changes in foreign claims. Overhead capital, including social overhead capital, should also be brought into the picture. Formally, we should also include additions to stocks of consumer durables in households but, since we are primarily concerned with the means of production of goods and services which enter into the national accounts, we leave them out of the picture. We might also note in passing that investment in human capital, which leads to qualitative improvements in human factor inputs through, for example, education and health care, is of some importance for future productive potential.

That the process of capital formation pervades throughout all sectors and sections of the economy is reflected in the papers which follow. As well as dealing with investment in manufacturing and mining, the paper on housing reflects the important contribution made by building and construction to total capital formation and particularly to its cyclical pattern.

Real *net* capital formation is a more difficult notion to pin down operationally and still more difficult to quantify. It involves us in conceptual difficulties which are easier to specify than to solve. In his paper on the south-west metal mining industry, Christopher Schmitz wrestles with just these problems and, while his actual estimates may be open to question, there can be little disagreement that he provides a vivid illustration of the difficulties involved in attempting to translate these difficult concepts into practice. In principle, real net capital formation is essentially capital formation over and above that which is required for 'keeping capital intact'. The importance of qualitative improvements in capital goods over time and estimating capital consumption, which in practice is much more a function of technological obsolescence than of physical wear and tear, needs to be estimated. With long-lived assets such as buildings it is also difficult to ascribe values to capital consumption for particular time periods.

## The process of capital formation

The process of capital formation is most easily analysed by considering individually its three major elements: *saving*, the *financing function*, and the act of *investment* itself. However, it is important not to ignore the inter-relationships among these elements. For example, just as a greater availability of savings facilitates higher levels of investment, so vigorous investment activity may stimulate saving by creating more profitable opportunities for individuals' portfolio investment. Conversely, a lack of saving may put a ceiling on the opportunities for investment activity and *vice versa*. Moreover, both saving and investment are conditioned by the efficiency of the financial mechanism. Finally, the financial system in turn will develop in response to the activities of savers and investors. So the development of a local capital market can both facilitate the financing of activities in that area and can in turn provide a convenient local outlet for savings.

## Saving

Saving represents a sacrifice of current consumption in order to free resources for conversion into capital goods with the object of increasing consumption opportunities in the future. It is an essential requirement for capital formation (except to the extent that capital goods can be imported and financed by foreign borrowing; but this is not likely to account for more than a modest proportion of a country's capital formation). In classical theory the level of saving and also the level of investment spending is determined by the rate of interest. The equilibrium rate of interest is, of course, that which exactly balances the amount of saving with the amount entrepreneurs wish to borrow for investment - a clear illustration of the inter-dependence of saving and investment.

Post-Keynesian othodoxy regards the level of income (ie the ability to save) as being the major determinant. But Keynesian theory deals essentially with the short-term determination of savings, investment and hence the equilibrium level of income. In considering the process of economic growth we are interested in the level of society's savings in the longer term. The long-run savings ratio may depend on several factors, among the most important of which are:

1 demographic factors, especially the relationship between the number of retired people (who may be assumed to be net dis-savers) and those of working age (who are generally net savers).

2 the distribution of income. Saving may be affected by egalitarian measures which redistribute income away from those with a high marginal propensity to save and toward those with a high marginal propensity to consume. Counteracting this factor, however, may be the increasing importance of contractual savings, which now form the bulk of personal saving in the UK.

So far we have considered only personal savings. The importance of corporate saving for the purpose of financing investment (the corporate sector is, in fact, characterised by high internal finance ratios) and also public sector saving, ie the surplus of revenues over expenditures, must also be recognised. If the demographic factors and egalitarian measures mentioned earlier combine to produce a stagnant or declining personal savings ratio, capital formation and continued economic progress may come to depend on public sector saving and, possibly, investment.

## The finance function

In a subsistence economy the functions of saving and investment are simultaneous - they amount to the same thing. Thus the finance function does not arise. However, in an exchange economy which is characterised by a high degree of specialisation of function there is a need for a mechanism by which the funds of large numbers of surplus units (or savers) may be channelled toward businesses which wish to finance capital projects on a scale which is increasingly beyond internal sources of finance (that is, toward deficit units).

Thus the function of the financial system is to transform the relatively small surpluses of large numbers of savers, whose time horizons are typically short and whose major concern is capital safety and liquidity, into large-scale, long-term, risky projects. This has been achieved by increasing the spread of knowledge about investment opportunities, the provision of brokerage and other services and especially by the growth in the number and variety of claims issued by a growing range of financial institutions. The rise in the importance of financial intermediaries has been a major feature of the economic and financial development of advanced countries. Not only do they facilitate the channelling of a given amount of savings into investment but also, by widening the number and variety of financial services (eg life assurance, specialist portfolio management) they have contributed to an increased flow of saving. There appears to be a high income-elasticity of demand for financial services.

The increasing importance of contractual savings, noted earlier, is testimony to the role played by financial intermediaries, both in altering the public's savings habits and in eliciting higher levels of savings.

If the financial system performs its task efficiently, the cost of the resources employed within it will be more than offset by the reductions in the real cost to businessmen of seeking out investment funds and to individuals in searching for profitable outlets for savings. Financial development renders society's savings both industrially and geographically more mobile.

The financial development of today's industrialised economies was primarily a response to growing demands for financial services on the part of savers and investors, that is, it was a demand-following phenomenon. It is unlikely, however, that less developed countries can afford to wait for a financial mechanism to evolve in this way. Hence they are faced with the need to shoulder the resource cost of establishing a supply-leading financial system if they wish to increase and mobilise their national savings for the purpose of stimulating growth and development.

## The act of investment

Finally, there is the act of investment itself, the commitment of resources to the production of capital goods, by which capital takes on a specific form.

The determinants of investment spending have received a great deal of attention from economists. This is mainly because consumption spending and the level of savings are assumed to *depend* on the level of income while (apart from government expenditures) investment is regarded as a largely autonomous factor which plays a major role in *determining* what the level of income will be.

Much of economic theory relating to the determinants of investment spending is concerned almost exclusively with the motivation of profit-maximising entrepreneurs. However, for a fuller picture, account must be taken of the increasing role of the public sector in the provision of goods and services for sale and also in house building. Investment decisions in this sphere may reflect primarily non-economic factors (eg the eradication of slums) or political considerations may be important or deliberate contra-cyclical investment may be authorised to speed economic recovery. Thus, to the extent that public authorities are of increasing importance in establishing the level of total investment, the theories of the determinants of investment require modification.

Further, there is the gradual replacement of entrepreneurial by managerial capitalism, the separation of ownership from control and the corresponding divorce of reward from risk-taking. In the modern world the large corporation accounts for an increasing proportion of economic activity. Along with these changes has gone the need to redefine the goals of the firm. Profit maximisation is no longer an adequate assumption and there is an increasing tendency to emphasise sales maximisation, corporate growth and, perhaps, the maximisation of managerial utility functions in which profit plays a subordinate role to other factors such as status. Since there remains a profit constraint, however, the managerial revolution must not be overstated. Managers must ensure that their company's share price (which is governed by dividend or earnings expectations) does not fall to a level which might preclude the raising of additional finance or else lead to a take-over bid or even a shareholders revolt.

These factors and also the fact that corporations rely heavily on internal sources of investment finance (undistributed profits), have all tended to reduce the emphasis put on the role of the rate of interest, which has occupied the centre of the stage in theories of capital and investment. Indeed it is now believed that the *availability* of funds rather than the terms on which they may be borrowed is the more important factor, even in the case of private house-building, which one might expect to be interest-elastic but tax relief is a complicating factor in this sector. Expirical evidence on the importance of interest rates is mixed but the general conclusion would seem to be that the rate of interest does help to explain changes in investment expenditure, especially over the longer term, but that the rate of interest is of subordinate importance to another factor, variations in the level of output.

There is a broad agreement that some form of accelerator model, which relates changes in desired capital stock to previous changes in the level of output, is most useful in explaining much of the behaviour of investment in fixed capital, especially in the shorter term. Such a model needs to be suitably adjusted to take account of time lags and the existence of excess capacity in the industry concerned. The principle refers to capital *outlays*, of course, and not to actual changes in capacity (failure to recognise this point has in the past led to seemingly disappointing empirical tests on the ability of the accelerator principle to predict investment). Thus account must be taken of the fact that lack of capacity or skilled labour in the capital goods sector may delay or frustrate investment decisions. This is reinforced by evidence that capital goods tend to be rationed by a lengthening of order books rather than changes in price.

Having dealt in turn with the components of capital formation it is important to emphasise again that they interact closely with one another and are in fact facets of a single process. It is, as we have seen, a process whereby the economy's potential for the production of goods and services in the future is increased by the release of resources from current consumption and their investment in the capital stock. This comprises far more than simply plant and machinery and buildings, which directly yield a flow of consumption goods and services; it also involves a substantial network of overhead capital, as well as the resources which are invested in the improvement of the human factors of production themselves. Economic progress has in the past been closely bound up with augmentations of capital in all its forms. The papers which follow deal with capital formation in certain individual sectors which have contributed to the progress achieved in the United Kingdom since the onset of the industrial revolution.

# AVAILABILITY OF CAPITAL IN THE WEST OF ENGLAND WOOLLEN INDUSTRY

Kenneth Ponting

'It is a generally accepted premise', wrote Peter Mathias, 'that there was no overall shortage of savings for productive investment in eighteenth century England'[1] because 'there were enough rich people in the country to finance an economic effort far in excess of the modest activities of the leaders of the Industrial Revolution'.[2] This position certainly applied in the West of England wool textile trade carried on in Gloucestershire, Wiltshire and north Somerset and would have been a natural result of a century of steady business. The visual effects of this prosperity still show in the fine houses the clothiers built which remain to give architectural distinction to the area. Moreover, in general 'many devices were employed for economizing in fixed capital (such as renting buildings, converting existing buildings and plant, hiring power, drawing credit from raw material suppliers): fixed capitals were very modest in relation to short term credit needs'.[3] The West of England woollen industry and in particular the financial accounts of the Clark family bear this out. However, as T S Ashton argued, 'industrial capital was its own chief progenitor' so even if capital was available it was possible to start with very little and expand on self-generated money. The young Clark brothers borrowed £499 from a rich uncle and did the rest themselves.

RATE OF GROWTH OF CAPITAL OF VARIOUS INDUSTRIAL FIRMS

| | Year | Capital £ | Average rate of growth per year (per cent) |
|---|---|---|---|
| Pleasley Mill | 1790 | 5,000 | 15.30 |
| | 1804 | 36,000 | |
| Gott & Wormald (Leeds) | 1792 | 20,000 | 13.73 |
| | 1815 | 397,000 | |
| J & T Clark (Trowbridge) | 1804 | 1,634 | 18.65 |
| | 1825 | 59,258 | |
| J Foster & Co (Black Dyke Mills) | 1834 | 11,185 | 16.10 |
| | 1867 | 1,463,155 | |

1 Francois Crouzet, ed. *Capital formation in the industrial revolution* (Methuen, 1972) p. vii.

2 Moses M Postan, 'Recent trends in the accumulation of capital', *Economic History Review*, V (1935) 1-12.

3 Crouzet, *Capital formation*, p. viii.

For the West of England woollen industry we have only one good set of business records but evidence will be offered later to suggest that the Clarks were not unique. For the moment it is worth comparing the Clarks' position with other textile firms elsewhere in the country. Included in a chart of the rates of growth of capital of various industrial firms there is information about four firms in the wool textile trade (see table on previous page).[1] The similarity is interesting and could be taken as suggesting that risk capital required a return of something like four times the basic interest rate as exemplified, for example, at that period in the rate of return on Consols.

The main capital cost for late eighteenth century manufacturers was the acquisition of a mill. Two different approaches were possible; if the firm had been long in the trade and had the money, a mill was built. Many fine examples of mills of c 1800 can still be seen. If the clothiers had little money or were just starting business they could rent premises, either a part of a mill built by someone as a speculative investment or more often a simple small shed or workshop. Most of the successful firms in the West of England began in this way.

To understand the rapid growth in the capital of J & T Clark, the history of the firm needs to be set out. In 1801 John Clark, who combined his business as a clothier with being the first pastor of the Tabernacle Church, lent his young nephew, also called John, £499 to start business on the understanding that his other nephew Thomas should join as a partner when he came of age in 1804. In this way the firm began and it is from the date of the partnership that the business records survive.[2] Their first workshops were in Yerbury Street where they took a lease on a house in 1804. A later Trowbridge clothier, William Walker, reported, 'as the lads grew up they started cloth making in Yerbury Street. They started with one carding engine and a slubbing billey. My mother worked for them at this time. They had a blind man to turn the carding engine, named Shem Reed, and then got another carding engine and then got Ham Reed, the blind brother of Shem to turn that engine, and so they got on and left Yerbury Street for Duke Street Mills'.[3] By 1816 Clark employed 25 men and 10 women.[4] John Clark lived at Yerbury House and his brother lodged with him.[5] They were actually given notice to quit in 1818 but a new lease must have been negotiated for they still occupied both business and workshop

1 Crouzet, ed. *Capital formation*, p. 199.

2 Robert P Beckinsale, ed. *The Trowbridge woollen industry as illustrated by the stock books of John and Thomas Clark, 1804-24* (Devizes: Wiltshire Archaeological and Natural History Society, 1951) p. xxxi.

3 Walker's journal is printed in Kenneth G Ponting, *The woollen industry of south-west England* (Bath: Adams & Dart, 1971) pp. 160-8.

4 *Minutes of Evidence taken before the Select Committee on the State of Children employed in the Manufacturies of the United Kingdom* (HC 397), *BPP*, 1816, III, 308.

5 Trowbridge Rate Book, Wiltshire Record Office (WRO) p. 206.

when the long leasehold was offered for sale in 1820 and again in 1824. By then they had moved the main part of their business to Duke Street, where the Clarks had bought a considerable property in 1814 and immediately ordered a steam engine, which cost £1000, from Boulton & Watt. As they also had to spend £600 on new machinery, they arranged for £2000 out of the purchase price of £2300 to remain in mortgage with the vendors. The payment of this by instalments was completed in 1821.

After some considerable trouble getting the previous tenant out, Clarks finally got their steam engine working in March 1815 to produce power for their new workshop which contained the carding, scribbling and tucking machinery. The building was insured for £800 and the machinery for £1000. The engine and boiler was only insured for £100. A year later the insurance on the machinery was increased to £1400. The other workshop contained only jennies and other hand-worked machinery.[1] In 1815 and 1816 Clarks enlarged the site by further purchase of land to the north where they made a reservoir for the steam engine and added other buildings.[2] Duke Street remained the centre of the firm's expansion until the end of the nineteenth century.

From 1826 to 1841 financial figures relating to the firm are missing but from 1842 until 1895 there is a complete series available.[3]

| Year | Capital (ie money in trade) | Profit |
|---|---|---|
| 1842 | 62,658 | 1,922 |
| 1843 | 63,871 | 8,956 |
| 1844 | 72,920 | 8,562 |
| 1845 | 80,114 | 909 |
| 1846 | 80,024 | 2,395 |
| 1847 | 78,102 | 268 |
| 1848 | 74,447 | 6,107 |
| 1849 | 74,541 | 3,160 |
| 1850 | 76,608 | 2,529 |
| 1851 | 77,486 | 2,633 |
| 1852 | 74,213 | 3,621 |
| 1853 | 76,113 | 4,886 |
| 1854 | 77,690 | 3,590 |
| 1855 | 79,162 | 1,831 |

1 Beckinsale, ed. *Trowbridge woollen industry*, p. xxv.

2 This account of Clarks business comes from my thesis 'The decline of the woollen industry in the Trowbridge and Bradford-on-Avon area in the nineteenth century', MA thesis, University of Bristol, 1974. For a good account of the Clarks, see also Kenneth Rogers, *Wiltshire and Somerset woollen mills* (Edington: Pasold Research Fund, 1976)

3 WRO 927/60 and 64.

| Year | Capital (ie money in trade) | Profit | Interest | Total Profit + Interest |
|---|---|---|---|---|
| 1856 | 76,289 | | 2,733 | |
| 1857 | 77,880 | | - 1,047 loss | |
| 1858 | 74,843 | | 2,970 * | |
| 1859 | 81,537 | | 4,248 * | |
| 1860 | 84,402 | | - 3,390 loss | |
| 1861 | 80,845 | | 1,095 | |
| 1862 | 80,930 | | 1,503 | |
| 1863 | 82,451 | | 2,763 | |
| 1864 | 84,179 | | 2,742 | |
| 1865 | 85,395 | | 3,051 | |
| | | Profit | Interest | Total Profit + Interest |
| 1866 | 93,075 | 402 | 2,785 | 3,187 |
| 1867 | 93,661 | 906 | 2,849 | 3,755 |
| 1868 | 95,374 | 516 | 2,873 | 3,389 |
| 1869 | 93,782 | 133 | 2,803 | 2,936 |
| 1870 | 87,368 | 1,703 | 2,096 | 3,799 |
| 1871 | 89,323 | 3,740 | 2,875 | 6,615 |
| 1872 | 89,644 | 1,209 | 3,164 | 4,373 |
| 1873 | 90,697 | | 194 | 194 |
| 1874 | 88,052 | | 99 | 99 |
| 1875 | 84,954 | | 1,374 | 1,374 |
| 1876 | 81,944 | | 1,247 | 1,247 |
| 1877 | 75,560 | | 2,055 | 2,055 |
| 1878 | 68,130 | | 853 | 853 |
| 1879 | 66,368 | | 2,166 | 2,166 |
| 1880 | 65,721 | | 1,299 | 1,299 |
| 1881 | 64,301 | | 1,287 | 1,287 |
| 1882 | 63,059 | 621 | 2,528 | 3,149 |
| 1883 | 60,256 | 2,680 | 2,411 | 5,091 |
| 1884 | 62,344 | 430 | 2,493 | 2,923 |
| 1885 | 62,149 | 2,965 | 2,489 | 5,454 |
| 1886 | 64,655 | 640 | 1,940 | 2,580 |
| 1887 | 64,093 | 1,510 | 2,564 | 4,074 |
| 1888 | 65,176 | 1,080 | 2,607 | 3,687 |
| 1889 | 65,709 | 2,185 | 2,619 | 4,804 |
| 1890 | 67,582 | 255 | 2,703 | 2,958 |
| 1891 | 67,562 | 277 | 2,006 | 2,283 |
| 1892 | 67,020 | 249 | 827 | 1,076 |
| 1893 | 48,478 | | (salary only) | |
| 1894 | 36,642 | | 747 | 747 |
| 1895 | 35,208 | - 2,067 loss | 1,416 | - 651 loss |

* partly paid as interest

Thus between 1825 and 1842 there was some expansion but nothing comparable to what had happened between 1804 and 1815. But the picture of steady progress is confirmed by the figures given in the 1833 factory enquiry report where John Clark said he employed 160 to 170 people in his factory and 800 to 900 outside.[1] From 1842 to 1868 the amount of

1 *First Report of the Commissioners for Enquiring into the Employment of Children in Factories, 1833* (HC 450), *BPP*, 1833, Bl. 94/95.

capital used in the business increased but the profit figure got steadily worse. From 1868 until the series ended in 1895 there is a steady decline in capital with little or no profit. The heavy writing off of capital during the years 1893, 1894 and 1895 suggest that losses during earlier years had been considerably greater than those actually shown in the accounts. The reasons for this decline do not concern us here, although it should be mentioned that it was typical of the trade of the area as a whole. Many firms gave up business but the Clarks, partly at least because they thought they owed it to their workers, continued to trade.

Nonetheless, adequate capital remained available for new development. In 1862 Clarks built Studley Mills which still stand, a power loom shed was added in 1865 and a further three-storied block to take machinery moved from Duke Street in 1885.

The history of the Clarks was not unique and although we have no financial records it is clear that at least two other firms in the town of Trowbridge, Salters and Stancombs, both followed similar lines. Judging from the evidence that we have, the comparison with Salters would seem to be remarkably close. The traditional date for the beginning of the firm is 1769 but this is probably a little too early and it may have been taken from a surviving pattern book beginning then, at one time in the possession of a descendant of William Walker who later controlled Salters for many years. This pattern book is now owned by the firm but there is nothing in it to connect it with Salters and the trade is far too extensive to fit with other facts known about the early days. The founder was Ephraim Salter and they were operating successfully by 1800.

The origin of Ephraim Salter is not completely certain because he was a Baptist so there is no baptismal entry for him. He was probably the son of Job Salter, a hosier (that is, a knitter of stockings) of North Bradley.[1] We know of Job through the sworn examination of his son John, also a hosier, taken for poor law purposes at Trowbridge, where he was living in 1764, and preserved in the parish records. To connect John and Job with Ephraim we must use notes left by Canon Jackson and now in the library of the Wiltshire Archaeological Society. Members of the Salter family were living in his parish of Farleigh Hungerford in the 1840s and it evidently intrigued him that these comparatively humble people should be cousins of a very rich clothier in a neighbouring town. Briefly, Jackson shows that Ephraim had two brothers, one, called William, a stocking weaver, kept the Talbot Inn at Farleigh and the other was called Job. The mention of the hosiery trade and the existence of brother Job makes it fairly certain that Ephraim was the son of Job Salter of North Bradley. Jackson also recorded the legend that Ephraim began at Trowbridge as a tailor without sixpence. But the first fully authenticated fact we know about him is that he was married at Trowbridge to Margaret Wills on 23 June 1772. He was then described as of the parish of St James, so it may be that his tailoring activities began at Bath and that marriage brought him back to his home area.

1 WRO 212A, section 34: agreement with Job Salter of St James', Bath, to employ the poor of Box. Also WRO 712: Poor Law Examination. I owe these references to Mr K Rogers.

The progress of the Salters' business can be inferred from the Trowbridge parish rate books[1] as not only houses and other buildings but also stock in trade was rated. Ephraim was first assessed in 1775 at a penny-farthing. Rating at that time was organised rather curiously according to modern ideas. A piece of property was assessed as a small sum, a little house paid fifty half-pennies and the owner of a big one fifty sixpences. In the following year Salters' name was associated with Dunn - no doubt the Joseph Dunn who had been the witness at his wedding - and the assessment was raised to two pence. This partnership, later augmented to Dunn, Salter & Dunn by the addition of Joseph's son William, continued until 1794 according to the rate books but deeds show that the firm was dividing some property that it owned early in 1792. Between 1780 and 1790 Ephraim Salter was also rated separately so he evidently ran some section of his business independently of the Dunns. As clothiers, Salter and his partners were moderately prosperous but by no means of the first rank.

Although there is again no baptismal record, Ephraim Salter's only son Samuel must have been born about 1778. The firm was first designated as E Salter & Son in the 1802 rate book and it is significant that its progress into a business as large as any in the town dates from this period. From two pence in 1802 their rating rose in 1803 to threepence half-penny, in 1805 to fourpence half-penny, in 1807 to ninepence and in 1812 to a shilling and in 1815 to 1s 8d. It certainly seems likely that they had factory space elsewhere than in the Home Mill site which must have been rented to make such a large trade possible in these early days. Father and son had obviously taken advantage of the new cassimere (fine twilled cloth) trade but there is no sign that they had suffered when that trade declined. In 1792 Ephraim Salter bought the house in Fore Street, until recently used by the Westminster Bank. Samuel bought the very fine house almost opposite in 1810. It is one of the best of many excellent clothiers' houses in Trowbridge. Father and son were now important figures in the town. Samuel invested much money in property, buying farms at Copp Hill and Farleigh Hungerford. He also put money in the local Salamander Insurance Society. He was a benefactor of the Back Street (the Emmanuel) Baptist church and its Sunday School and at his death left five almshouses for aged members of the council. Canon Jackson spoke of him rather condescendingly as a very civil and respectable man who never gave himself airs.

Ephraim Salter died in 1812 at the age of 74, leaving his son in full control of the business. Although Samuel married, he never had any children. His nearest relatives were the children of his only sister, Margaret, who married William Stancomb, another Trowbridge clothier. He appears to have singled out one daughter, Sarah, who married Jessie Gouldsmith, as his heir. Samuel died on 26 December 1850 at the age of 72, leaving it was said, £350,000. His widow Mary, who was about fifteen years his junior, remarried one William Reeves and she survived until 1870.

1 WRO 206.

In 1816 Salter employed 39 men and 66 females, giving a total of 105 workpeople, and he was the largest employer in Trowbridge at the time.[1] By the time of the 1833-4 factory enquiry, Salter's business had increased in size and in his deposition of 3 June 1833, Samuel stated that he employed about 150 people at the factory and 450 outside.[2] This figure would suggest that business had increased in size by approximately 50 per cent between 1816 and 1833. On the basis of the people employed in the factory, Clarks were slightly the larger but there was not a great deal of difference. The fact that Clark said he employed so many more people outside probably means that he was counting many weavers who only worked partly for him. Generally speaking, however, the two firms do represent similar conditions and both show how capital could be generated inside the trade.

The later history of Salters also confirms the position at Clarks. Following the death of Samuel Salter, the business passed under the control of the Gouldsmiths family. According to William Walker's journal, 'The Gouldsmiths: before they came to Trowbridge they were woollen cloth merchants in London, and were related to Mr Salter, and joined him partnership'.[3] Their own period of control can be divided into two parts, the first before the fire of 1862 and the second after. The first period was mainly one of consolidation. For a time Salters were the largest mill in the town, having, round about 1860, surpassed Clarks. At the time of the fire they were said to employ 500-600 operatives, with a capital of around £50,000, but either the number of operatives was too high or the capital too low.

As a family the Gouldsmiths kept very much to their business and family interests. Indeed, when Jessie Gouldsmith the elder, then retired and living in Clifton, died in 1871, the local newspaper could only say of him 'highly respected cloth manufacturer. He had amassed great wealth but being a man of retiring habits he took little or no share in public matters. In the circles in which he mixed he was much esteemed and by his death we have lost one of the best exhibitors at our local flower show'.[4]

The 1862 fire was an important event in the annals of the town as well as of the firm. After giving a very lurid account of the fire, the local newspaper concluded an article which ran for several columns with the words: 'The situation for a large factory is not exactly in the centre of a circle of dwelling houses and shops and much anxiety is felt lest it should be erected in the same spot'.[5] It is clear from the reports that follow in the newspapers that soon the anxiety about having the mill in the centre of the town quite disappeared. Indeed, there was considerable doubt whether it would be rebuilt at all; the

1 *BPP*, 1816, III, 308.

2 *BPP*, 1833, Bl.94/95; also *BPP*, 1833, XX, Bl.92. See also *Supplementary Report 2nd part* (HC 167), *BPP*, 1834, XX, Bl.102, 1011. Also see *BPP*, 1833, Bl.94/95 for interesting evidence by employees.

3 Walker's journal in Ponting, *Woollen industry*, p. 162.

4 *Trowbridge Advertiser*, 21 December 1871.

5 *Trowbridge Advertiser*, 12 December 1862.

elder Gouldsmith apparently did not wish to do so and he retired from the business. The Haywards, who had been associated with the firm, did not play any part in the rebuilding and moved to another smaller mill in the town. For a time a leading firm of Stroud clothiers were involved but quite quickly the Gouldsmiths, this time the two sons of Jessie the elder, were in complete control. This period was another of consolidation and it can be followed reasonably well from the local newspapers.[1]

Jessie Gouldsmith the younger, in particular, has left a number of records and was famous for his gorilla, which accompanied him to the mill in his coach in the morning. Unfortunately, both of the younger Gouldsmiths died comparatively young. When Jessie died in 1885 the local paper reported that he had been incapacitated for several years but that four hundred people were employed. 'In 1885 Salter's Home and Duke Street Mills were in the market through the death of Mr W & J Gouldsmith', William Walker wrote in his journal. 'They were offered by auction but drew no bid and I bought Home Mill buildings - Applegates Yard - the wool house and paddock between the back of the house in Applegates Yard and Home Mill buildings at the auction, after which I made an offer of £13,000 for the Home and Duke Street Mills which was accepted. I afterwards bought the stock of wool yarns and cloth and machinery, as it stood, the total amount of this purchase was £48,888. Before my action the mills were likely to be stopped and sold, but my buying them they went on working without an hours stop'.[2]

William Walker continued to run the business until early in the twentieth century when he handed over to his son. In 1896, the same year as the Clarks became a limited company, Salters attempted a public flotation with 1000 shares of £1 each and £30,000 4½ per cent mortgage debentures on offer. But this attempted flotation was not successful, suggesting that the business was not worth the money that Walker set upon it. Indeed, the failure of the flotation and the overall picture gained from the newspaper reports and local traditions confirm that during the twenty years 1876 to 1896, the fortunes of Salters followed much the same course as those of Clarks.[3]

In summary, the history of these two firms shows that in the early years of the nineteenth century, money could be made quite fast in the the West of England textile trade; that during the middle decades of the century it was possible to maintain a steady business; but that the last twenty years were very difficult. During these years many firms went out of business but it must be emphasised that this was not a new phenomenon. Firms had been going out of business regularly right from the beginning of the century and the success of Clarks and Salters, as

1 *Trowbridge Advertiser*, 16 May 1863.

2 Walker's journal in Ponting, *Woollen industry*, p. 165.

3 The information regarding the failure of this flotation came from my father who began working at Salters in 1899.

of a few other firms, such as the Stancombs and the Lavertons of Westbury, the Marlings of Stroud, the Players of Minchinhampton and the Tuckers of Frome, stand out against a background of many failures. It would probably be reasonable to rank successes as about 10 per cent of the total.[1] Thus the main theme of this essay is that at the beginning of the nineteenth century money was available and could be self-generated and that throughout the century shortage of capital was never a major problem. The industry's general decline must therefore be found in other directions; in the failure to adapt to fashion changes and the growth of the wholesale making-up trade. The adaptation to these new fashion trends would not have needed any major capital equipment but required the more difficult capability of changing the habit of mind built up over several decades.[2]

1 It was usually said in the local newspapers that they declined business; comparatively few went bankrupt.

2 In preparing this paper I am deeply indebted to Dr Julia de Lacy Mann for much help and advice and to Mr Kenneth Rogers for assistance in sorting out the early history of the Clarks and Salters.

# CAPITAL FORMATION AND TECHNOLOGICAL CHANGE IN SOUTH-WEST ENGLAND METAL MINING IN THE NINETEENTH CENTURY

Christopher Schmitz

## I

This paper surveys some of the problems involved in examining capital formation in the non-ferrous metal mining industry of Cornwall and Devon before 1914. It has little to say about the channels through which that capital flowed; the tin and copper smelting companies, mine supplies agents and public share issues.[1] It concentrates on the methodological difficulties of assessing capital structure with reference to technological change in a declining industry.[2]

In discussing past trends in the capital structure of any industry a number of general problems arise, in particular the definition of the term 'capital'. However, as suggested by Stanley Chapman, 'the problems associated with the calculation of capital formation in the economy vary from one industry to another'.[3] Each industry has its peculiarities and its own problems with evidence. It is the major argument of this paper that the mining industry requires special treatment; that the concepts of capital stock as applied to the majority of manufacturing industries are inappropriate in the case of mining. Study of capital formation in south-west metal mining will require an appreciation of the unique economics of the industry.

The starting point is a brief analysis of the economic cycle of mineral exploitation, with reference to conditions in the south-west, followed by discussion of methodological problems encountered in calculating the industry's capital stock through time. Looking at a selected range of indicators, such as use of steam plant, consumption of timber and other mine materials, some estimates of capital formation can be presented. The underlying theme throughout is that representing the relationship between technological change and capital requirements, as measured in changing capital-output ratios. It is to be doubted whether the data at present available on the industry in the south-west will ever permit of such a sophisticated level of capital-output ratio analysis as attempted for the United States by Creamer, Dobrovolsky and

1 Little has been written on this aspect of capital formation in mining but see Denys Bradford Barton, *History of tin mining and smelting in Cornwall* (Truro: Barton, 1967) pp. 71-6, 127-30 for detail of smelting company interests in mining finance; also Roger Burt, 'The London mining exchange 1850-1900', *Business History*, XIV (1972) 124-43.

2 From 1850 to 1914 total value of copper and tin ores mined in Cornwall and Devon (expressed in 1914 prices) fell from £2.27 million to £0.82 million.

3 Stanley D Chapman, 'Fixed capital formation in the British cotton industry 1770-1815', *Economic History Review*, 2nd series, XXIII (1970) 235.

Borenstein.[1] Forming part of a broader study of the economic history of metal mining before 1914, this paper suggests a number of avenues to be pursued and tentatively warns of the pitfalls that could be encountered.

II

The economic cycle of mineral exploitation imposes a pattern which constrains the development (and ultimate decline) of mining wherever it has taken place in the world. Stated briefly, this theory suggests that mining starts at shallow depths, working relatively rich or mineralogically simple ores, but as time passes (the length being a function of rate of working and size of deposit) ores of decreasing value must be pursued to greater depths. This fact has the most profound consequences for both the nature of capital formation and technological change in the industry. Changes in capital structure and technology relate largely to what has been termed 'the struggle against rising costs'. In a study with that sub-title, an American survey of the 1930s suggested that 'the history of mineral exploitation is a record of a struggle against increasing natural difficulties. It is a commonplace that the richer and more accessible of the known deposits are attacked first. As these are exhausted, operations proceed to poorer and less accessible deposits, and the physical conditions become progressively more difficult'.[2] The pattern apparent in the United States mining industry in the early decades of the twentieth century was also to be seen in the south-west of England during the nineteenth.

Mining for tin in the west of England is almost certainly one of the longest-established industries in the British Isles and by the late eighteenth century, it could be argued, had reached a 'mature' stage in the cycle of exploitation.[3] There was no significant opening up of new tin areas after the mid-eighteenth century. Such development as followed until the sharp decline of production in the 1890s occurred through working at greater depths, often under previously-worked copper deposits.[4] The copper mining industry, on the other hand, had only

1 Daniel Creamer, Sergei Dobrovolsky and Israel Borenstein, *Capital in manufacturing and mining: its formation and financing* (Princeton: National Bureau of Economic Research, 1960).

2 F G Tryon and Margaret H Schoenfeld, 'Mineral and power resources' in *Recent social trends in the United States* (New York: McGraw-Hill, 1933) p. 64.

3 George R Lewis, *The Stannaries: a study of the English tin miner* (Cambridge, Mass: Harvard UP, 1908); Barton, *Tin mining*.

4 The classic example is Dolcoath mine, Camborne, which made the transition from copper to tin in the 1850s (Barton, *Tin mining*, pp.111-13).

become significant after a period of rapid growth in the 1770s and 1780s and until the 1840s continued to develop new areas of exploitation in the south-west.[1] Thereafter, until the catastrophic collapse of the late 1860s, copper mines tended to pursue increasingly poor minerals to greater depths.[2] Such mines as survived continued this trend.

In the late 1770s Dolcoath copper mine, one of the leading producers, was working to a maximum depth of 540 feet from surface[3] and the average depth of mines then would have been around two to three hundred feet. By the late 1860s Dolcoath, having become the leading tin producer, was down to 2000 feet[4] and by 1914 had reached its ultimate depth of over 3300 feet, a west-country record.[5] Through the 1870s and 1880s it was common for mines to be working at depths of 1500 feet or more.

When going deeper the mining companies usually encountered ores of decreasing metal content. In the early 1880s the English mining engineer Robert Hunt estimated that the average value of copper ores raised in Cornwall and Devon had steadily declined over the previous century; from around 12½ per cent in the 1770s, to about 9 per cent in 1800, to around 7 per cent by 1850 and by the 1880s such mines as were still producing copper were working ores of just over 6 per cent metal content.[6] With tin ores the decline was less dramatic. At the peak of its tin-producing career, in the early 1890s, Dolcoath mine was working ores averaging 3½ per cent metal content. By 1914 the average was down to just over 1¼ per cent.[7]

The net effect of mining at increasing depths and extracting ores of diminishing metal content was that the industry had to adopt improved methods of underground mining, haulage, pumping and surface milling and, related to this, it had to increase its capital-output and capital-labour ratios. The most successful mines in the long run (that is, those that enjoyed a sustained period of relatively profitable production after the general collapse of tin prices after 1894) were those which adopted advanced techniques and adopted long-term planning of mineral

1 As late as 1844 a new copper lode was discovered less than 100 feet down, near Tavistock. Worked as Devon Great Consols mine, this was the largest copper producer in Britain from then until the end of the century (John C Goodridge, 'Devon Great Consols: a study in Victorian mining enterprise', *Transactions of the Devonshire Association*, XCVI (1964) 228-68).

2 Denys Bradford Barton, *History of copper mining in Cornwall and Devon* (2nd edition, Truro: Barton, 1968).

3 Thomas R Harris, *Dolcoath* (Camborne: Trevithick Society, 1974) p. 11.

4 Harris, *Dolcoath*, p. 56.

5 Harris, *Dolcoath*, p. 91.

6 Cited in William Y Elliott et. al. *International control in the non-ferrous metals* (New York: Macmillan, 1937) p. 374.

7 Harris, *Dolcoath*, p. 98.

stocks in the ground as well as, in some instances, combining with other mining companies to operate in larger units of production. All of these activities would have had a fundamental effect on the nature of capital formation in the industry.

Study of past trends in capital formation in the metal mining industry of the south-west, it can therefore be argued, can be directed not only towards helping improve aggregate national estimates of capital formation but also can be of interest within its own right. Only if we appreciate the changing capital requirements of the mining industry in relation to changing market conditions and technological frameworks can we fully understand its development and decline.

Whilst much thorough research has been done into the history of metal mining in south-west England, for example in the voluminous writings of Bradford Barton,[1] of A K Hamilton-Jenkin[2] or Cyril Noall,[3] most of this has been cast in an antiquarian mould, cataloguing the development of underground workings, of mining machinery and the lives of the men in the industry. For studies of capital formation in mining we have to turn to the other side of the Atlantic and the pioneering work of Israel Borenstein in his 1954 publication, *Capital and output trends in mining industries 1870-1948*.[4] This research was further consolidated in the 1960 National Bureau of Economic Research publication, *Capital in manufacturing and mining: its formation and financing*, by Creamer, Dobrovolsky and Borenstein. With a substantial introduction by Simon Kuznets, this latter work helps provide us with the kind of conceptual framework we will need in examining the metal mining industry; in looking at its capital formation and in an examination of the relationship between capital-output trends and changing patterns of technology and organisation.

III

In general terms there are great difficulties in assessing capital formation; locating full and reliable data, defining capital, distinguishing net from gross capital formation, circulating from fixed capital, of estimating depreciation and the rate of retirement of assets.

At first approach the task of estimating changing capital stock in nineteenth-century Cornish and Devon metal mining seems to be set with insurmountable difficulties. Data of investments in mining are

1 *History of tin mining*, *History of copper mining* and *Essays in Cornish mining history* (2 vols. Truro: Barton, 1968-71).

2 *The Cornish miner* (3rd edition, Allen & Unwin, 1962); *Mines and miners of Cornwall* (16 vols. Truro: Barton, 1961-67; Penzance: Federation of Old Cornwall Societies, 1969-70).

3 *Levant* (Truro: Barton, 1970); *Botallack* (Truro: Barton, 1972); *The St Just mining district* (Truro: Barton, 1973).

4 National Bureau of Economic Research, occasional paper 45, New York, 1954.

generally imperfect and information on the use of plant such as steam engines, ore-dressing machinery and rock drills is not easily obtained. There are no aggregate estimates of capital in the industry before the first world war; even the 1907 Census of Production has little to say about metal mining in Britain. It merely records the total value of output and an estimate, provided by the industry, of the value of materials used in the year.[1] This source suggests that whilst output in 1907 from United Kingdom mines 'other than coal and iron' was worth around £1.63 million, the imputs of raw materials were valued at just £0.43 million. Resolving this figure with a concept of capital, circulating and fixed, within the industry is not an easy task. The figure of £0.43 million presumably represents the value of hardware consumed (timber, machinery, explosives etc) plus the cost of leases, power, fuels and royalties. It does not seem to include the labour imput, although this is not clear. Overall it would seem best to treat it as the non-labour element in a gross addition to circulating capital and an increment to accumulating fixed capital. What proportion of this sum constitutes the latter is not clear. The proportion would have varied through time; with technological change the ratio of fixed capital formation to circulating capital within any one year's expenditure would have increased. As for the 1907 imput estimate, perhaps 60 to 80 per cent represented circulating capital and the residue an increment to longer-term fixed investment like the purchase of new plant.

Given the uncertainty over estimates of total fixed capital in the industry, it is desirable at this stage to introduce a control to the subsequent calculations in the form of an extrapolation back from known output levels to possible levels of capital formation, via estimates of capital-output ratios provided by Creamer, Dobrovolsky and Borenstein.[2] Using estimates of this ratio provided for the United States during the period 1870-1890, we can obtain a range of values for fixed capital in relation to output. From this we can also derive estimates of working capital, again using ratios proposed by the American study. One objection to this method is that capital-output ratios, and indeed the definition of capital, appropriate to the United States may not be applicable to Britain, even in the same period. It may be true that mining in the United States was less labour-intensive than that in the United Kingdom, in accordance with the Habakkuk thesis,[3] but as this paper will show subsequently, in many ways British

1 *Sessional papers, House of Commons* (Cd.5254) 1910, CIX, 254. In fairness it should be noted that it was not the original intention of this census to construct estimates of capital formation as such.

2 *Capital in manufacturing and mining*, pp. 73-5.

3 Hrothgar J Habakkuk, *American and British technology in the nineteenth century: the search for labour-saving inventions* (Cambridge UP, 1962), which basically suggests that US manufacturing industry was typified by labour-scarcity and so tended to develop labour-saving technology, in contrast to Britain where a surplus of labour inhibited such developments.

metal mining was also becoming less labour-intensive over time and the gap may not have been particularly large. In addition there was a strong cultural link between mining in the south-west and in the United States; Cornish mining methods were widely adopted in the early copper and lead workings of Michigan and Wisconsin. Even where technological change did take place it usually built on Cornish systems.[1] For these reasons it is felt that the application of a band of capital-output values to recorded south-west mineral output between 1850 and 1914 is not entirely inappropriate. Creamer, Dobrovolsky and Borenstein suggest the fixed-capital to output ratio in United States mining (copper, lead and zinc) varied from 0.57:1 to 1.46:1, and rising marginally on trend through the period.[2] In recognition of the lower level of capital-intensity in Britain and the average level for the

Table 1

Capital in south-west mining in the nineteenth century

| £,000 annual average | copper output | tin output | total | fixed capital | | working capital | |
|---|---|---|---|---|---|---|---|
| | | | | i | ii | i | ii |
| 1850-59 | 1081 | 658 | 1739 | 696 | 1217 | 174 | 435 |
| 1860-69 | 782 | 830 | 1612 | 645 | 1128 | 161 | 403 |
| 1870-79 | 324 | 815 | 1139 | 456 | 797 | 114 | 285 |
| 1880-89 | 100 | 782 | 882 | 353 | 617 | 88 | 221 |
| 1890-99 | 13 | 499 | 512 | 205 | 358 | 51 | 128 |
| 1900-09 | | 573 | 573 | 229 | 401 | 57 | 143 |
| 1910-14 | | 825 | 825 | 330 | 578 | 83 | 206 |

All values expressed in current prices.
Fixed capital = accumulated total of fixed investment allowing for depreciation and retirement of assets (i and ii = lower and higher ranges).
Source of output values: *Mineral statistics of the United Kingdom.*

1 Arthur C Todd, *The Cornish miner in America: the contribution to the mining history of the United States by emigrant Cornish miners* (Truro: Barton, 1967); John Rowe, *Hard-rock men: Cornish immigrants and the North American mining frontier* (Liverpool UP, 1974).

2 *Capital in manufacturing and mining*, pp. 73-5. Their breakdown of capital formation in US copper, lead and zinc mining is, in 1929 prices:

| | copper mining | | | lead and zinc mining | | |
|---|---|---|---|---|---|---|
| | 1870 | 1880 | 1890 | 1870 | 1880 | 1890 |
| Capital ratio to output | 0.76 | 1.74 | 0.82 | 0.77 | 0.74 | 0.75 |
| Of which, plant | 0.63 | 1.46 | 0.64 | 0.58 | 0.57 | 0.59 |
| Of which, working | 0.13 | 0.28 | 0.18 | 0.19 | 0.17 | 0.16 |

United States working out at around 0.75:1, the band applied to Britain has limits of 0.4:1 and 0.7:1. Creamer, Dobrovolsky and Borenstein's estimates of circulating capital are also utilised. They estimate this to vary from 0.13:1 to 0.28:1 and so for the purposes of this calculation the limits for the British industry have been set at 0.10 and 0.25. From these admittedly arbitrary parameters we can obtain the benefit of an indication of the kinds of levels of capital formation we can expect to find in the south-west metal mining industry in this period.

We thus derive estimates that suggest that the stock of fixed capital in south-west metal mining was between £690,000 and £1.2 million in the 1850s, fell to around £200,000 - £350,000 in the depression days of the 1890s and rose again with rising tin prices and renewed mining activity just before 1914 to around £330,000 - £580,000, expressed in current prices.

Beyond this generalised level of discussion, some of the technical problems associated with constructing estimates of capital formation fortunately never really arise in this area. There is simply not sufficient data to enjoy a level of sophistication in analysis anticipated by Simon Kuznets, when he warns the potential researcher in the field of some difficulties encountered:

> Should we take capital gross or net of accumulated depreciation, confine it to real assets or include financial assets; and if the latter, should all financial assets be included or should they be limited to some 'working minimum'? Should the denominator of the capital-output ratio be gross value of output, or net value added (ie net of cost of materials and fuel), or net income originating (ie compensation of productive factors net of all payments to other industries)?[1]

Our analysis could hardly ever be that sophisticated, given the basic lack of data. In the subsequent discussion, after expanding on some of the methodological problems unique to the mining industry, it is proposed to examine a number of indicators of capital formation in the industry, such as numbers of steam engines with an estimation of their value, extent of underground development, levels of employment, and then generally to corroborate the broad estimates presented above in table 1. Further than this, only a great deal of painstaking research in the capital structure of individual mines, gleaned from the contemporary trade press, such as the *Mining Journal*, published weekly from 1835, and other sources might in due course provide a fuller picture of change in the capital structure of the industry.

## IV

The first problem encountered, and perhaps the major one, is that of adequately defining 'capital' in the context of the mining industry. It is not suggested that the term does not require careful definition in other industries but that conventional concepts of capital, land and

1 *Capital in manufacturing and mining*, p. xxiv.

labour as factors of production cannot be taken straight from discussion of manufacturing industry and applied without alteration to the mining sector. With the latter, some items in the productive process will clearly come under the heading capital: steam-engines, pumping machinery, rock-crushers, buildings, water-leats, etc. The difficulty arises when one turns to the basis of the operation, the minerals in the ground. Are they to be considered as land or capital resources? It can be argued, as illustrated more fully below, that a mineral deposit when first discovered by a mining company constitutes a land factor, until the point at which they start developing its potential. Once the company starts sinking shafts, driving underground levels and generally making the deposit ready for production, the accumulated sum of the relevant labour and capital imputs consumed in establishing the productive **infra-structure** represents a capital asset which must be taken into account. This is an area where study of capital formation in mining needs to be conducted with due regard to the peculiar economics of the industry.

Other minor problems exist, such as the danger of under-recording the capital value of buildings or plant constructed by company labour (ie not charging labour at an economic rate).[1] However, the major problem remains with categorising mineral deposits at various stages in the life of a mine.

Some text-book definitions of capital do not help much, for instance one which runs: 'durable goods such as buildings, plant and machinery' together with the circulating capital 'stocks of raw materials and semi-finished goods, components etc'.[2] Others are of greater value to this discussion. Richard Lipsey suggests: 'everything man-made which is not consumed for its own sake but which is used up in the process of making other goods'.[3] This would allow the inclusion of mine shafts, underground levels and other features of the underground productive **infra-structure,** together with the more tangible assets like plant and surface buildings.

Whilst with Lipsey it is worth noting that he adds the suggestion that mineral resources, as 'free gifts of nature', should be regarded as land factors of production.[4] This view does not seriously conflict with the argument of this paper, inasmuch as mineral deposits in the ground, undiscovered or discovered, but *undeveloped*, can usefully be

1 Sidney Pollard, 'Fixed capital in the industrial revolution in Britain', *Journal of Economic History*, XXIV (1964) 150, suggests that buildings etc installed internally by a company are often entered with ***book value*** equal to the cost of raw materials, even wages as well, and so the true capital value accruing is lost. He further suggests this could be true of mining, in the sinking of pits, for example.

2 Graham Bannock, Ronald Baxter and Richard Rees in *Penguin dictionary of economics* (Harmondsworth: Penguin, 1972) p. 55.

3 Richard Lipsey, *Introduction to positive economics* (2nd edition, Weidenfeld & Nicolson, 1966) pp. 58-9.

4 Lipsey, *Positive economics*, p.58.

regarded as a land resource, as much as fertile soil or timber in the forest. Once prepared for production, however, the mineral deposit being opened by shafts, the asset assumes a higher value.[1]

Another difficulty in assessing capital in mining is noted by J D Gould, in looking at 'non-monetised investment'.[2] He cites the examples of agricultural improvements such as ditch or hedge construction wrought by peasant labour, where a labour imput is converted into a fixed capital asset. This example is easily extended to the accumulated product of underground excavations wrought by mine labour. In general, Gould suggests, this problem in under-estimating the capital value of accumulating labour services becomes more pronounced the more labour-intensive the system we are looking at or, in broad terms, the further back in time we go.[3] In these terms an examination of the nineteenth-century mining economy of Cornwall and Devon would present more problems than would the highly mechanised Cornish tin industry of today.

In order to understand the applicability of the concept of underground mining development as a form of capital accumulation, it is necessary to look at the way in which mines were typically opened up for production. Once a mineral deposit had been located, or reasons for its presence suspected, if it were near the surface the mining company merely had to sink a shallow pit in order to exploit the ore-body.[4] If however, as was increasingly the case in nineteenth-century Cornwall and Devon, the ore-body was located, or suspected to lie, at hundreds of feet from surface, then an elaborate system of shafts and levels would be required in order to reach the lodes and assess their productive potential. This process is described by a mid-nineteenth-century writer:

> Before commencing operations it is essential to ascertain the bearing or direction of the vein . . . these things may be ascertained by sinking a few shallow pits upon the lode, and, when the required information is obtained, the vein may be explored either by sinking upon its course from the surface, or by forming a horizontal passage to intersect it, commencing from some neighbouring valley. When the shaft has been sunk to the depth of about sixty feet, a horizontal gallery or level is cut in the lode, both towards east and west, say, the ore and materials being raised by a common windlass. It is evident that by thus sinking shafts a hundred yards from each other, the

1 This concept can be extended to the case of soil; once ploughed and limed, the fields assume a higher value and cease to be a purely land resource, having assumed a certain capital status.

2 *Economic growth in history* (Methuen, 1972) p. 123.

3 *Economic growth in history*, pp. 123-4.

4 The classic example of this type of development was the vast, shallow copper ore-body of Parys Mountain, Anglesey, opened in the 1760s. See John R Harris, *The copper king: a biography of Thomas Williams of Llanidan* (Liverpool UP, 1964).

> first gallery or level may be prolonged ***ad libitum***. But while this horizontal work is going on, the orginial or engine shaft is sunk deeper; and at a second depth of sixty feet, a second level, or horizontal gallery is driven east and west . . . this may be continued to any depth. It will be evident that these shafts and galleries divide the lode into solid rectangular compartments, each of which is, in dimension, three hundred feet in length, by sixty feet in height. These masses of three hundred feet are again subdivided by small perpendicular shafts into three parts; and by this management the lode is finally divided into masses called *pitches*, each sixty feet in height, by about thirty-three feet in length.[1]

This system of underground excavation described by John Leifchild was common to almost every working mine when any depth was attained and resulted in the division of the veins, or lodes, into blocks (the older mining term being 'pitches'). A survey of the longitudinal section of any medium to large Cornish mine of the nineteenth century will display a characteristic 'grid' pattern, with shafts from surface crossing an elaborate pattern of underground levels and shafts, 'blocking-out' the lode.[2] This development was essential to the working of a deep mine and necessarily involved a considerable investment; first of all for a 'dead period' of perhaps two years before the ore bodies could be brought into production and a return shown and then continued investment in maintaining existing shafts and roadways and in further extending the mine both laterally and at depth to maintain the supply of ore-bearing ground. The amount of this underground development could be extensive. Within five years of its opening in 1844, Devon Great Consols copper mine had driven a total of 5853 fathoms, nearly seven miles, of vertical and horizontal underground workings.[3] At the Gwennap Consolidated copper mines it was estimated that between 1818 and 1838 a total of 37,330 fathoms of levels and 18,000 fathoms of shafts were excavated, a total of nearly 63 miles of underground workings, according to the manager, John Taylor.[4]

The above generalisations about the pattern of mine development do conceal a couple of important points. Shafts being sunk in Cornish mines before 1914 were commonly sunk 'on the underlie', that is at an incline, following on the ore-body from surface, and thus the 'dead period' was often eliminated. Also, mining was often a fairly continuous activity, with mines starting at shallow depths and then

1 John Leifchild, *Cornwall: its mines and miners* (Longmans Green, 1857) pp. 138-42.

2 A good example of such a mine plan is to be found in Harris, *Dolcoath*, p. 96.

3 Leifchild, *Cornwall*, p. 150.

4 Quoted in Leifchild, *Cornwall*, pp. 150-1.

progressing in stages, perhaps under different companies, to greater depths. In this way many mines overcame the need for extensive capital formation prior to production from ore-bodies at depth. The most spectacular exceptions to this rule were those mines abandoned at depth and then re-opened with great expense in pumping, re-timbering and in generally re-establishing the productive infra-structure. Great Wheal Vor tin mine, near Helston, was re-opened in this period 1853-60, having been sunk to a depth of over 1700 feet in the previous working of 1836-45. To 31 December 1857 the total cost of the re-opening was £294,769, against sales of ore valued at £120,852. By 1860, and the demise of the venture, the total loss was estimated at over £207,000.[1] Examples of losses of this kind abound in the history of metal mining[2] and add a further dimension of uncertainty to calculations of capital formation in the industry. To what extent can capital formation which ultimately proves to be of little or no avail in productive terms, be included?

The kind of productive infra-structure described became more necessary the deeper and more dispersed the mineral deposits were located, a situation becoming increasingly common in the south-west by the mid-nineteenth century. It became more necessary in particular with the growth of the concept of a 'permanent mine'. This idea developed inasmuch as companies refrained from mining ores as soon as they were discovered. Instead it was increasingly common for mines to 'block out' ground so as to have on hand anything up to two or three year's reserves of ore at the current rates of production.[3] As soon as this shift was made in the industry, from predominantly shallow mines, producing as and when they found the ore, to one in which deeper mines were stocking up a solid reserve of unworked ore, a new capital requirement entered into the situation. By the 1850s the system of medium-term reserves was becoming commonplace. Amongst many examples that could be cited is the case of Wheal Exmouth lead mine, Christow, Devon. There, it was reported in September 1855 that the company had about 6000 tons of ore blocked-out underground, equivalent to 3½ years' reserves at the current mill output rate of 150 tons a month.[4] Indeed, so common was the 'permanent mine' system by the 1890s that exceptions to the rule invited special comment. The antiquated Blue Hills tin mine, at St Agnes in Cornwall, when finally closing in 1896 after 27 years' continuous working, was described as

1 Barton, *Tin mining*, pp. 100-7.

2 The uncertainties of the industry prompted Sir William Forbes to comment, 'I regard mining as a very deep species of gambling, whereby there has probably been more lost upon the whole than gained' (*Memoirs of a banking house* (London, 1860) p. 39).

3 The essence of a permanent mine was that with two or three year's known reserves in stock, a mine could indulge in a degree of forward planning, for instance intensifying exploration programmes if the ore-bodies showed signs of depletion.

4 Christopher Schmitz, *The Teign Valley lead mines* (Sheffield: Northern Mine Research Society, 1973) p. 61.

'a curious mine working quite on the old-fashioned principle; such tin as was discovered was taken away at once'.[1]

As mining companies depended more and more on steady and predictable production levels in the short-run, allowed by the continual reserves system, the total amount of underground development of a semi-permanent nature in the south-west tended to increase. This underground development, it is argued, was just as importance in the production of minerals as were the more concrete capital assets of steam-engines and milling machinery at surface. Any estimates of capital formation in the industry must take account of this, despite problems relating to valuing its non-monetised imputs and in reconciling non-productive investment, as in the case of Wheal Vor, to total investment and capital accumulation.

V

Beyond the general problem of identifying 'capital' in the mining industry, there is the need to define and assess the extent of depreciation and retirement of assets. In any construction of estimates of changing capital formation over time there has to be an allowance for running repairs on plant or the cost of replacement once the useful life of that plant is ended. In the mining industry these calculations resolve into two issues: the physical replacement and repair of plant (as in manufacturing industry) and an assessment of the life of mines (and therefore a return to the discussion of capital values and depreciation of the less tangible assets contained in the underground productive infra-structure).

Assessing rates of depreciation in plant is not entirely straightforward. Figures on the life of machinery and on the cost of maintaining it through its working period are not always readily available in a useful form. Also, when is a particular piece of plant in need of replacement? How can the value of maintenance work done as running repairs by company personnel in the course of their ordinary duties be assessed? These kinds of problems compound the difficulty of the economic historian's task.

Taking one stock item of metal mining plant in the nineteenth century, the steam engines used for pumping, winding and driving milling machinery, it is possible to derive an indication of rates of depreciation and asset retirement in relation to their expected life-spans and repairs effected in-service. There is abundant information in the contemporary mining press,[2] in manuscript mining records[3] and

1 Barton, *Tin mining*, p. 224.

2 In the *Mining Journal* (1835-); Lean's *Engine Reporter* (1810-); the *West Briton* (1810-); the *Royal Cornwall Gazette* (1800-); the *Sherborne Mercury* (1736-).

3 Extensive collections in the Cornwall County Record Office, Truro; Devon County Record Office, Exeter (especially the Bedford collection); the Royal Institution of Cornwall, Truro; Messrs Harvey & Company Ltd, Hayle, Cornwall (foundry records).

in other miscellaneous sources[1] of the engines in use in the mines of the time, although it would take much painstaking research to yield any meaningful data of the type required. For the purpose of this discussion a few well-documented engines will be taken as a sample, although it could be argued that these will not constitute a random cross-section of all engines: the better-documented examples will usually be those of exceptional life-span. This criticism cannot be wholly countered, although it does seem fair to state that such background research as has been conducted indicates that the life-spans and maintenance histories of the better-documented engines was broadly similar to that for a much broader spectrum of engines.

The main point to emerge from an analysis of these steam engines is that they enjoyed a long working life by the standards of present-day industrial plant. It was not uncommon for a Cornish beam pumping engine to be in use for sixty, eighty or even a hundred years, on one or more different sites, since there was always a thriving market in second-hand engines. A few examples can be cited. A 70 inch cylinder pumping engine built by the St Austell Foundry in 1852 worked in three different mines until 1883 and was then sold to the Severn Tunnel Company, on whose site it remained in working order until the 1960s.[2] Another 70 inch cylinder engine, built by J E Mare and Company of Plymouth in 1853 was first put to use at Wheal Exmouth lead mine, Devon, and then moved to two other mines in the south-west, to a South Wales purchaser in 1876, only to return to a Cornish mine, where it was advertised for sale in 1898. Its subsequent fate is unknown.[3] A 70 inch pumping engine built by the Harvey and Company works at Hayle survived even longer; installed at the Prestongrange Colliery, East Lothian, Scotland in 1874, it was still at work in 1951.[4] One of the most famous Cornish engines to survive is that on Robinson's Shaft, South Crofty mine, Camborne. Built in 1854 by the Copperhouse Foundry of Sandys, Vivian and Company at Hayle, it was first erected at Alfred Consols mine in the same year. It subsequently moved to Crenver and Wheal Abraham in 1864. Another move came in 1881, to Tregurtha Downs mine, near Marazion, where it remained until 1903. It was then transferred to its present home at the still-active South Crofty tin mine, where it was pumping water from a depth of over 2000 feet until 1955.[5] Casting the net further afield, a recent listing of surviving steam plant provides an indication of the age-range of a broad spectrum

1 Denys Bradford Barton, *The Cornish beam engine* (2nd edition, Truro: Barton, 1966); Thomas Lean, *On the steam engines in Cornwall* (Truro: Barton, 1969); Edmund Vale, *The Harveys of Hayle* (Truro: Barton, 1966); Nicholas Von Tunzelmann, 'Technological diffusion during the industrial revolution: the case of the Cornish pumping engine' in Ronald Max Hartwell, ed. *The industrial revolution* (Oxford: Blackwell, 1970) pp. 77-98.

2 Barton, *Beam engine*, p. 61.

3 Barton, *Beam engine*, p. 61, and Schmitz, *Teign Valley*, pp. 49, 70.

4 Barton, *Beam engine*, p. 62.

5 Barton, *Beam engine*, pp. 79, 243-7.

of engine types and uses. Of the 159 engines recorded as still working in the early to mid 1970s, in a range of industries throughout Britain, 14 were less than fifty years old, 63 were from fifty to seventy years of age, 57 were between seventy and ninety years old, and 25 were in excess of ninety years of age.[1]

In connection with assessing the working life of steam plant it is worth bearing in mind the general point made by Tibor Barna that it is easy to underestimate the life of industrial equipment. Barna suggests that the life of plant is often considerably longer than normally assumed, so that the nature and rate of technological change (slower in the nineteenth century than the twentieth) may be a factor in rates of depreciation.[2] J D Gould extends this idea by suggesting that a general rule can be postulated; that certain kinds of technology generate certain rates of depreciation. For example, modern high-consumption technology has an inbuilt and necessary element of accelerating obsolescence.[3]

Applying these concepts to steam plant and other mining technology, we can see a model of technological change as related to depreciation of capital assets emerging. This suggests that as time passes, coming nearer to the present, individual items of plant last less time. The modern electric motor or internal combustion engine, operating at higher revolutions and subject to faster obsolescence, will only be in use for perhaps ten years. The high-pressure horizontal or compound steam engine of the late nineteenth century might have lasted for an average thirty years or so. The Cornish engine of the early and mid-nineteenth century, working at low speeds, 6-10 revolutions a minute was common, and subject to a range of simple repairs and modifications, may have lasted for an average fifty to sixty years. A long-term quantitative study of steam technology would be required to verify this thesis and improve on the quality of these figures. For the moment, the theory in its crude form is sufficient to warn us of the dangers of applying strictly twentieth-century depreciation criteria to the technology of an earlier period. In broad terms the evidence also serves to indicate that the rate of depreciation of the capital stock in mining tends to accelerate towards the end of the nineteenth

1 Robert A Buchanan and George Watkins, *The industrial archaeology of the stationary steam engine* (Allen Lane, 1976) pp. 138-74.

2 'On measuring capital' in Friedrich A Lutz and Douglas C Hague, *The theory of capital: proceedings of a conference held by the International Economic Association* (Macmillan, 1961) pp. 92-3.

3 *Economic growth in history*, p. 122.

century.[1]

The second major area of concern in relation to depreciation and the retirement of assets is that involved in reconciling the value of investment in the underground infra-structure to the life of individual mines. In economic terms, the inherent long-run diminishing returns obtaining in mining activity dictate that all underground investment must be written off at some time. There are examples of mines which operated for longer than average periods. Levant mine, near Land's End, was in continuous operation from 1820s until the 1930s. Dolcoath mine was at work even longer, from around 1798 (or earlier) until the 1920s. In all cases, however, mines have to close as the non-replaceable mineral deposits are exhausted within the given technology-related cost-structure and in doing so write off a proportion of their accumulated capital stock. Whilst some of the underground plant, such as pumps, piping and tramway rails, might be retrieved in normal circumstances, the larger part of underground fixed investment, represented by the capital value of levels, timbering, shafts and shaft supports, will be lost forever. Even if a mine were re-opened within a short while much of this would have to be re-established; abandoned mines soon fill with water, rotting timbers and causing levels and shafts to collapse.[2]

In manufacturing industry a large proportion, if not all, of the plant on hand at the end of operations could be expected to have some resale or scrap value. In mining this was rarely true. There exists, therefore, the problem of accounting for depreciation and retirement of the non-recoverable elements in the capital structure, in relation to the ultimate and inevitable closure of individual mining concerns. Two factors complicate this issue. First, it was often the case that mining companies were not able to anticipate impending closure for more than very short periods before the end of operations. This would be particularly true of mines of the non-permanent type, operating with little or no ore reserves in the ground. Thus, it would not necessarily follow that they would make allowance for depreciation so as to write-off a proportion of the assets before closure. Secondly, for mines that

1 In this context Deane and Cole note that the ratio of net to gross capital formation in Britain declined from about 0.8:1 in the 1860s to 0.5:1, or lower, in the 1950s. In making allowance for depreciation, net capital formation's declining ratio to gross formation reflects the increasing importance of technological obsolescence and asset retirement through time (Phyllis Deane and William A Cole, *British economic growth 1688-1959: trends and structure* (2nd edition, Cambridge UP, 1967) pp. 265,307). In allowing for depreciation in the period 1856-1913, Feinstein's estimates of life expectancy for plant and buildings (40 years and 100 years, respectively) seem reasonable (Charles H Feinstein, *National income, expenditure and output of the United Kingdom 1855-1965* (Cambridge UP, 1972) p. 201).

2 In the re-opening of Wheal Vor in 1853-60, the deeper workings (under water for 8 years) were found to be 'in a very disordered state' (Barton, *Tin mining*, p. 104).

had been working for long periods, the accumulated stock of capital had in many cases already depreciated fully, at least in the eyes of the company; helping perhaps to account for the apparent low costs in the industry and the extent to which mines seemed to work at a loss for long periods.[1]

One way in which mines nearing the ends of their lives dealt with depreciating assets, if they could foresee closure, was to run down their replacement or maintenance of underground and surface equipment and so anticipate to a certain extent the writing off of stock. Cook's Kitchen mine, adjacent to Dolcoath at Camborne, had a long career spanning the period from the late eighteenth century until final closure in 1895. During this period it was never very profitable and at the same time acquired a reputation for its poor state of repair and the antiquated state of its machinery. The state of the plant and the underground workings deteriorated rapidly in the later years of the mine's life and by the time of closure in 1895 one contemporary source described the main pumping engine as 'simply a wreck, for the bob was broken, the nozzle patched in at least a dozen places, the cylinder was full of holes. Directly the engine was stopped and cooled down, the principal part of the engine almost dropped off'.[2] The mines' inspectors might reduce the incidence of accidents caused by poor maintenance of steam plant and other equipment but they could not eliminate it completely in an industry where declining prices and increasing foreign competition forced mine owners to think increasingly in terms of running down plant.[3] The long-lived Levant mine, near Land's End, is a good case in point. There, by the end of the first world war, the management were anticipating closure

1 Wilfred Salter notes, 'How often does one see the statement that an industry can produce cheaply because its capital equipment is fully depreciated' (*Productivity and technical change* (2nd edition, Cambridge UP, 1966) p. 61). For the year 1837 the tin industry estimated its net loss on 68 major mines as over £60,000 (Barton, *Tin mining*, p. 70). Mines could continue to make losses for long periods, eg Cook's Kitchen mine, Camborne, paid only two dividends between 1809 and its closure in 1895 (Barton, *Tin mining*, pp. 131, 219).

2 Barton, *Tin mining*, p. 219.

3 This was reflected in growing numbers of fatalities in tin mining, both in relation to numbers in the industry and to fatalities in other UK mines. Barton, *Tin mining*, p. 244, cites the following figures:

Fatalities per 1000 men employed underground

| Year | in Cornwall | in all UK mines |
|---|---|---|
| 1902 | 1.15 | 1.37 |
| 1903 | 1.45 | 1.35 |
| 1904 | 2.00 | 1.35 |
| 1905 | 3.70 | 1.52 |
| 1906 | 3.63 | 1.42 |
| 1907 | 2.39 | 1.46 |
| 1908 | 2.78 | 1.47 |

and so as well as laying off a large proportion of the work-force, started a policy of accelerating the depreciation of their capital stock. In this particular instance the consequences were grave. The lack of maintenance on a man-hoisting device, the 'man engine', precipitated 31 miners to their death in October 1919.[1]

In an aggregate sense depreciation of capital stock in mining was rapid through the second half of the nineteenth century. As indicated in table 1 (p. 30 above), the level of output in the industry of the south-west fell from around £1.7 million to £0.5 million in the last fifty years of the nineteenth century, expressed in current values. At the same time the amount of capital stock in the industry must have fallen dramatically, with mines closing and plant being sold for scrap. There was a passing revival in the fortunes of tin mining in the early years of the twentieth century with rising prices and many new mines opened. This would have boosted the amount of capital formation in the industry temporarily. Overall, however, the picture from the mid-nineteenth century to the first world war is one of continuing decline and of rapid rates of depreciation of capital stock, the latter falling in value by perhaps a half or more.

## VI

The next stage in this study is to attempt some broad estimates of aspects of capital formation in the south-west mining industry. One way of doing this is to take numbers of steam engines, consumption of mine timber, for example, and to construct estimates of the value of these items. Moving on to the more difficult area of the underground productive infra-structure, it might be acceptable to look at numbers employed in the construction of these underground structures and a consideration of the value of the labour imput into this element of capital formation.

Starting with steam plant, an estimate of the number and types of engines in use in Cornish mines during 1838 was provided by the local geologist, William Henwood. He listed 245 engines at work,

1 Barton, *Tin mining*, pp. 258-9; Noall, *Levant*, pp. 99-117.

together with a breakdown of their type and size:[1]

Table 2

Cornish steam engines on mines in 1838

| | | |
|---|---|---|
| Pumping | less than 40 in cylinder | 47 |
| | 40 in but less than 60 in | 57 |
| | 60 in and over | 44 |
| | total | 148 |
| Whims, stamps[2] | less than 20 in | 45 |
| | 20 in but less than 27 in | 46 |
| | 27 in and over | 6 |
| | | 97 |
| | total engines | 245 |

This information, when allied with contemporary estimates of the cost of engines,[3] enables us to compile an approximate figure of their total value. Assuming, from the available information on costs, that an 18 inch cylinder whim cost, on average, £390 and a 70 inch pumping engine an average £1675, for example, then the total capital cost of the engines at work in 1838 was about £170,000.[4] To this would have to be added the cost of engine-houses, pit-work and other ancillary equipment, not usually included in the basic price. This might add at least a further 20 to 30 per cent to the total.

By 1865 a further picture is available of numbers and types of steam engines, provided by the mining share-broker Thomas Spargo.[5] He suggests that in that year there were 554 engines of all types in the south-west (table 3). One point of significance in his estimates is that there is a higher proportion of whim engines in the total than for 1838. The number of stamps engines had also increased relatively. Stamps and whim engines, were, on the whole, of smaller cylinder diameter and of lower cost than pumping engines. This counteracts the larger numbers of engines to a certain extent and after a survey of engine prices at the time, it was possible to calculate the total cost

1 Barton, *Beam engine*, p. 252.

2 Whim engines were used for hoisting purposes, stamps for crushing.

3 See, for example, Barton, *Beam engine*, pp. 52, 61, 67, 73-7, 279-81.

4 Calculated on the basis of average engine costs for median sizes and types in each category, weighted by size of category, then result multiplied by totals and aggregated.

5 Barton, *Beam engine*, p. 252.

Table 3

Cornish steam engines on mines in 1865[1]

| | | |
|---|---|---|
| Pumping | less than 40 in cylinder | 88 |
| | 40 in but less than 60 in | 127 |
| | 60 in and over | 58 |
| | | 273 |
| Whims | less than 20 in | 40 |
| | 20 in but less than 26 in | 136 |
| | 26 in and over | 8 |
| | | 184 |
| Stamps | 18 in to 24 in | 70 |
| Crushers, capstans and man-engines | 8 in to 36 in | 27 |
| | total engines | 554 |

of these engines at about £320,000.[2] As in 1838, a further 20 to 30 per cent would have to be added to this to represent the value of pitwork and other ancillary equipment. Overall, between 1838 and 1865, on the basis of these estimates, the total value of engines, pitwork etc would have increased from around £220,000 to £400,000. After 1865 the value of steam plant would have declined very rapidly, as the copper industry plunged into a depression from which it never emerged and the tin industry only survived until the 1890s when it, too, succumbed to falling market prices and foreign competition. The declining value of steam plant was reflected in the falling value of second-hand engines. Before 1865, with a fairly healthy mining market, the lively market in old engines maintained relatively high prices. In July 1862 the 70 inch pumping engine of Wheal Exmouth, Christow, was sold to Old Wheal Neptune, Perranuthnoe, for £1225, complete with two 10 ton boilers.[3] This compared with a common price-as-new at the time of around £2000. Commonly, engines were sold for around half their value as new. After the copper collapse of the late 1860s, however, the market was flooded with engines from abandoned mines and prices fell dramatically. In August 1866 South Carn Brea mine, Camborne was auctioned and the entire plant, including steam engines, went for

1 Barton suggests Spargo did not include every mine in his survey and that the true figure of steam engines was more like 650 for Cornwall and about 60 for Devon, an overall total of about 710. Barton further suggests this was the all-time peak figure for the area (*Beam engine*, p. 253).

2 Calculated as for 1838; see footnote 4, p. 42 above.

3 Barton, *Beam engine*, p. 61; Schmitz, *Teign Valley*, p. 70.

£900.[1] With depression in the tin market in the later 1870s prices fell even further. In January 1879 a 22 inch whim engine was sold at auction for only £9.[2] The rapid deterioration in the value of steam plant through the 1860s and 1870s is reflected in the falling capital in the mining industry; in relation to the rough estimates of table 1 (p. 30 above), declining from around £0.7 million - £1.2 million in the 1850s, to £0.4 million - £0.6 million by the 1880s.

The other major source of motive power in mines in the nineteenth century was provided by water-wheels. Unfortunately, full information on the extent and value of water-power in mining is not readily available, although this element in the fixed capital of the industry was certainly very important.[3] Barton has calculated that about 70 water-wheels were in use in Devon and Cornwall between 1816 and 1866 for pumping and a further 50 or so powering whims.[4] Costing about £300 to £500, including leats and other engineering, the total value of this plant would have been about £40,000 to £60,000.

Approaching the more complex problem of assessing the capital value of underground workings in mines, we can examine estimates of total materials consumed in the industry provided by some writers at the time. It is also possible to take the accounts of individual mines, where the equipment and materials used have been itemised. An assessment of labour imputs in relation to the construction of the underground infra-structure may also be employed in estimates of capital formation.

There are occasional valuations available of timber used in the south-west mining industry. Leifchild estimated that in 1834 the cost of timbering in Cornish and Devon mines was £50,947, in 1835 £64,563 and in 1836 £94,138.[5] Charles Lemon provided estimates for a longer

1 Barton, *Beam engine*, pp. 64-5. The engines were a 26 in pumper with pitwork, flatrods etc, a 24 in whim and a 30 in stamps with 68 heads.

2 Barton, *Beam engine*, p. 72.

3 Water power was more important than steam in Devon, with the high rainfall of Dartmoor, and reflects the low number of steam engines.

4 'Water-engines in Cornish mining' in *Essays in Cornish mining history*, I (Truro: Barton, 1968) pp. 167-8.

5 *Cornwall*, p. 155.

period:[1]

Table 4

Cost of timbering in Cornish and Devon mines
(including carriage), annual averages

| | £ |
|---|---|
| 1818-22 | 32,900 |
| 1823-27 | 50,700 |
| 1828-32 | 44,600 |
| 1833-37 | 57,800 |

Lemon also estimated that the total consumption of coal in mines during 1834 was 69,559 tons, which at around £1 per ton would be valued at about £70,000.[2]

The accounts of individual mines have been preserved in some instances and shed a brighter light on the extent of capital in the industry, as represented by materials consumed, cost of labour and miscellaneous items. Leifchild cites the case of the Gwennap Consolidated copper mines, the largest individual enterprise at the time, and its itemised cost sheet for 1836.[3]

Table 5

Cost sheet of Consolidated mines in 1836
(extracts)

| | |
|---|---|
| Total expenses | £102,007 |
| Details | £ |
| Tutwork bargains | 26,177 |
| Tribute | 25,030 |
| Agents' salaries | 3,343 |
| Carpenters, masons, smiths | 3,099 |
| Surface workers | 2,539 |
| Materials | 15,008 |
| Engine or water costs | 15,415 |

1 'The statistics of the copper mines of Cornwall' in Roger Burt, ed. *Cornish mining* (Newton Abbot: David & Charles, 1969) p. 78.

2 'Statistics', p. 76.

3 *Cornwall*, pp. 175-6.

Table 5 (continued)

| | | |
|---|---|---|
| | £ | |
| Expenses on ores | 7,803 | |
| Sundries | 1,872 | |
| Carriage & horses | 922 | |
| Medical expenses | 795 | |
| **Persons employed** | | |
| Agents | 28 | |
| Tutwork men | 441 | |
| Tributers | 392 | |
| Surface men | 335 | |
| Underground boys | 109 | |
| Surface boys | 327 | |
| Females | 755 | |
| Total employed | 2,387 | |
| **Materials consumed[1]** | | |
| Coal | 11,817 | tons |
| Candles | 113,916 | lbs |
| Gunpowder | 64,000 | lbs |
| Timber | 51,220 | feet |
| Pick & shovel hilts | 13,098 | dozen |
| Ropes | 977 | cwt |
| Chains | 3,474 | fathoms |
| Iron | 108 | tons |
| Steel | 135 | cwt |

Some of the items listed relate to circulating or working capital, others to fixed capital formation but in no cases is the distinction completely clear. As argued below, in the discussion of the labour element in capital formation, a large part of the tutwork or contract labour relates to the excavation of underground levels and shafts, that is the fixed productive infra-structure. Other items relating to fixed capital formation include the consumption of timber and perhaps a proportion of the iron and steel, in constructing underground levels and shafts. More difficult of definition is the role of gunpowder. It is used in the excavation of tunnels and shafts as well as in loosening the ore and so its use is a necessary part of the accumulating stock of underground excavations, of the productive infra-structure. Should it, therefore, be charged to circulating or fixed capital? Other items such as pick and shovel hilts, candles, ropes and the utilisation of tribute or ore-face labour are perhaps more readily categorised as elements in working capital.

1 This list of materials consumed represents merely a selection of a much fuller list, total value £15,008, contained in the original source.

An unusually detailed insight into the value of plant on a mine is provided in an inventory of Levant mine made in December 1871, when a new company took over control.[1] This list is extensive and includes items like:

20 in Man Engine (4½ ft stroke) with Boiler 9 tons, 2 Balance bobs, and 35 fathoms 6, 7 and 8 in rods with plates, caps, etc, £200
Water Wheel and launders, £15

64 Lifters and tongues, 7 tons 4 cwt at 4s 6d, £32 8s

40 Tin frames, £7 10s
4 Setts of Flat trunks, £3
Water Wheel, 4 Bolases buddles, Buddle House and Launders complete, £58

Tram road on Incline road, £2

2 Miner's Dials, £4 10s
Pitwork (Selected items, not individually valued)

Tramroad at the 190 left under water
Tram road Iron, 1450 fathoms, 20 tons, £50

Man Engine Shaft, rods, etc, £60
Skip road in Whim Shaft, £25

The total value of materials was estimated at £3432 16s 6d, this being at a time when the company was commenting on the fact that 'Everything had been allowed to get into a ruinous condition'.[2]

Examples of these kinds of inventories are not too uncommon in printed and manuscript sources but a great deal of research would be required before a fuller picture of the value of plant used in the industry could be assembled. Until then, there will be no clear way of verifying the estimates of capital in mining made on odd occasions by contemporary writers like Charles Lemon.[3]

1 Noall, *Levant*, pp. 34-5.

2 Noall, *Levant*, p. 35.

3 Lemon constructs some broad estimates of capital in, production of and costs of the Cornish copper mining industry in 1799:

| | cost | output | capital |
|---|---|---|---|
| Class I mines | £116,209 | £180,440 | £102,489 |
| Class II mines | £49,311 | £140,790 | £66,813 |
| Class III mines | £31,813 | £18,330 | £16,267 |

Lemon defines class I mines as numbering 10 and being 'old and deep'; class II number 7 and are 'newer profitable' mines; class III number 42 and are 'comparatively new'. Lemon notes, however, that he doubts the accuracy of these figures (Burt, *Cornish mining*, pp. 56-7). Also, the definition of 'capital' in this context is not clear.

Considering the highly labour-intensive nature of the nineteenth-century mining industry, it is necessary, when attempting any assessment of capital formation, to make allowance for non-monetised investment, already discussed in general terms above (pp. 33-6). That the industry was highly labour-intensive is beyond doubt. In the cost accounts of the Consolidated Mines for 1836 (table 5 above) a total of 2387 persons were employed, at a cost of £60,188, about 60 per cent of total costs. Charles Lemon expands on the issue by suggesting that the ratio of wages and salaries to gross expenditure in the Consolidated Mines in 1836 was 0.673 to 1, and in Fowey Consols copper mine, even more labour-intensive, 0.777 to 1.[1] In this productive framework, the accumulating value of certain labour services to fixed capital formation would be of primary importance.

The total number of men employed in the south-west mining industry, that is, for copper, lead and tin, rose from about 18,500 in 1841 to 35,000 (the peak figure) in 1861 and by 1911 had fallen to 7200 (table 6).

Table 6

Employment in Cornish and Devon metal mining[2]

1841-1911 (male)

(thousands)

| | copper | tin | lead | total |
|---|---|---|---|---|
| 1841* | 12.1 | 5.9 | 0.6 | 18.6 |
| 1851 | 16.8 | 12.8 | 3.3 | 32.9 |
| 1861 | 18.0 | 14.3 | 2.1 | 34.4 |
| 1871 | 2.7 | 10.6 | 1.5 | 14.8 |
| 1881 | 3.3 | 10.4 | 0.4 | 14.1 |
| 1891 | 1.4 | 9.7 | 0.1 | 11.2 |
| 1901 | 0.5 | 6.6 | | 7.1 |
| 1911 | 0.1 | 7.1 | | 7.2 |

*the 1841 census almost certainly seriously underestimates numbers in the industry

It should be indicated here that the non-inclusion of women workers relates to the fact that in south-west mines they were exclusively employed at surface, with children, in breaking, sorting and dressing ores.

1 Burt, *Cornish mining*, p. 67.

2 Decennial census reports 1841-1911.

In examining the labour element in the construction of underground workings, the structure of the male labour force needs to be analysed. Apart from those who worked at surface, the body of miners in the south-west were by tradition divided into two classes, tributers and tutworkers. The former, generally regarded as the more experienced miners, were not paid regular wages but worked for a previously agreed proportion of the value of the ores they raised to surface, the exact proportion varying in inverse relation to the value of the ores being worked. The value was assessed by the mine agents from time to time prior to the 'setting day', perhaps once a month or every three months, when new 'bargains', or tributers contracts, were offered by the company. The tributers were the 'face-workers' and were provided with an incentive to mine the ores very efficiently in order to maximise on the value of their particular 'bargain'. In contrast, the tutworkers were employed by the mining companies on the basis of a fixed wage in order to drive levels through 'dead ground', that is containing no mineral bodies, and generally to maintain and extend the underground workings.[1]

An assessment of the cost of tutwork labour, it is argued, will provide a rough-and-ready indicator of the value of labour services entering into provision of the underground productive infra-structure. This can be calculated from estimates of tutworkers' wages at various times, given in a range of sources, and from estimating the numbers of tutworkers employed from time to time.

An estimate of tutworkers' wages in 1836-7 gives the following figures:[2]

Table 7

Average monthly wages of tutworkers in 1836-7

| | £ | s | d |
|---|---|---|---|
| West of Penzance | 2 | 5 | 0 |
| Mid-Cornwall | 2 | 17 | 2 |
| St Austell district | 2 | 19 | 0 |
| Average | 2 | 13 | 8 |

In 1836 the prospering Consolidated mines could afford to pay more than the regional average, setting a standard tutwork rate of £3 11s 6d a month.[3] By 1865 tutwork wages had risen marginally in the south-west, the following figures being provided by the Kinnaird Commission on

1 See Burt, *Cornish mining*, pp. 20-5, 38-41, 133-92.

2 Hamilton-Jenkin, *Cornish miner*, p. 205.

3 Leifchild, *Cornwall*, p. 176.

conditions in British metal mines:[1]

Table 8

Tutwork rates in four Cornish mines, 1865

| | £ | s | d | per month |
|---|---|---|---|---|
| Providence mines, St Ives | 2 | 19 | 3 | |
| Wheal Margery, St Ives | 2 | 13 | 4 | |
| Wheal Reeth, St Ives | 2 | 19 | 10 | |
| North Levant, St Just | 3 | 0 | 9 | |
| Average | 2 | 18 | 3 | |

By the early 1870s, with a boom in tin mining, wages were again slightly higher. One source cites average monthly tutworkers' wages as being:

1872 £3 16s 3d; 1873 £4 1s 6d; 1874 £3 13s 7d; 1875 £3 10s 0d[2]

By 1882, Levant tutworkers were receiving £3 18s 6d a month.[3] Thereafter the distinction between tutwork and tribute seems to have grown weaker in the south-west, as more modern concepts of company structure and wage structures began to infiltrate from elsewhere in Britain. Overall, the sum of the evidence suggests average tutwork wages were around £2 14s 0d in 1836, around £2 19s 0d in 1865, about £3 16s 0d in 1872 and approximately £3 19s 0d in 1882. Expressed in terms of annual rates these are:

Table 9

Average annual tutworkers' wage rates, 1836-82

| | £ | s |
|---|---|---|
| 1836 | 32 | 8 |
| 1865 | 35 | 8 |
| 1872 | 45 | 12 |
| 1882 | 47 | 8 |

Data of numbers of tutworkers employed, unlike those for wages, are not directly available and have to be calculated from the total numbers of men employed (table 6) and an estimate of the ratio of tutworkers to total numbers of males employed, drawn from a number of

1 Question 7995, cited in Burt, *Cornish mining*, p. 181.

2 Burt, *Cornish mining*, p. 182.

3 Noall, *Levant*, p. 52.

published examples. In 1836 Consolidated mines, the largest south-western mining employer, had a total of 1604 men and boys at work underground and at surface. Of these, 441 were tutworkers, 27.5 per cent of the total (table 5). In the same year, the neighbouring United mines had 198 tutworkers, 29 per cent of the total 686 men and boys employed.[1] In 1837 Fowey Consols copper mines, near St Austell, employed 358 tutworkers from a total of 1381 men and boys, a proportion of 26 per cent.[2] By 1849 the same mine accounted for £16,347 tutwork wages, from a total male wage-bill of £38,560, a proportion of 42 per cent.[3] By this time the proportion of tutworkers in the male labour force at Fowey Consols seems to have increased and with higher tutwork monthly rates than for surface labour (about £2 19s 0d compared to £2 0s 0d) the proportion of wages account taken by the former would be correspondingly greater. From this and other data available it would seem that a reasonable estimate of the tutwork proportion of the total male labour force in mining was around 28 per cent.[4]

On the basis of these figures it is possible to suggest the numbers and total wage account of tutworkers in Devon and Cornwall from 1841 to 1881:

Table 10

Tutwork labour in the south-west, 1841-81[5]

| | Numbers ('000) | Total wages (£,000) |
|---|---|---|
| 1841 | 5.2 | 168.5 |
| 1851 | 9.2 | 325.7 |
| 1861 | 9.6 | 339.8 |
| 1871 | 4.1 | 187.0 |
| 1881 | 3.9 | 184.9 |

1 Leifchild, *Cornwall*, p. 173.

2 Leifchild, *Cornwall*, p. 179.

3 Leifchild, *Cornwall*, p. 178.

4 Mines in decline often employed higher proportions of tributers in order to reduce costs and so after the copper collapse of the 1860s it is likely that the proportion of tutworkers in the labour force declined significantly.

5 Wage rates from table 9 applied to employment figures thus: 1836 wage estimate to 1841, 1865 wage estimate to 1851 and 1861, 1872 wages to 1871, and 1882 wages to 1881. It must be noted that the 1841 employment figure is certainly an underestimate; see Leifchild, *Cornwall*, p. 172.

The sums generated in this calculation suggest that the value of labour imputs into the construction and maintenance of the underground productive infra-structure, apart from the actual mining of the ores, declined from around £300,000 per annum in the 1850s and 1860s to around £180,000 per annum by the 1870s and 1880s and probably falling further after 1890.

Aggregating the various estimates of capital formation in different areas of mining, presented in this section, it is possible to indicate a rough level of fixed capital provision (accumulated and accruing) at intervals through the nineteenth century:

Table 11

Fixed capital formation estimates for the Devon and Cornwall mining industry, 1820-65

(£,000)

| | c 1820 | c 1840 | c 1865 |
|---|---|---|---|
| Accumulated | | | |
| Steam plant | | 170 | 320 |
| Water power | | 50 | 50 |
| Total | | 220 | 370 |
| Accruing | | | |
| Timber | 33 | 58 | |
| Tutwork | | 169 | 340 |
| Total | | 227 | |

The limited value of these estimates suggest how necessary is further extensive research into the subject, difficult as this may be, given the uneven quality and survival of documentary material.

## VII

The broad pattern of capital formation has been indicated; a gradual rise to its peak in the 1860s, with general prosperity in the copper and tin mining economy, and then successive periods of collapse in mining, first in copper, later in tin, resulting in a steady decline in capital formation, with mines closing and assets depreciating rapidly. In the context of decline in the industry, the question of the relationship between technological change and capital formation assumes particular importance. As has been pointed out earlier in this paper, the south-west mining industry had to pursue ores of diminishing value to greater depths as the nineteenth century progressed. The capital requirements of such a mature mining field, with limited opportunities for discovery of fresh deposits near surface, would reflect the need for more extensive programmes of exploration and underground development to stock up larger quantities of low-grade ores. At the same time deeper mining would require more efficient and higher capacity pumping equipment; more complex or leaner ores would require more advanced and capital-intensive forms of milling and concentrating equipment at surface.

By the last quarter of the nineteenth century technological change in south-west metal mining was running at a significant level. In the words of L L Price, in a study of the industry's wages system written in 1891, 'Metallic mining is no longer . . . the hap-hazard pursuit of signs and tokens - deceptive or otherwise - that it once was . . . mere rule of thumb is being replaced by a body of scientific experience'.[1] Mining and milling methods were improving in step with the application of modern scientific theory to mining practice. Dolcoath introduced a traction engine to haul tin to the smelters in 1885, compressed air winches were employed in East Pool mine at about the same time and by the late 1880s a number of mines were using compressed air boring machines.[2] In 1890 a Parliamentary inquiry listed 21 mines in Cornwall and 4 mines in Devon with a total of 60 such machines.[3] Overall, metal mining in Britain was certainly becoming less labour-intensive, as crude male-labour productivity statistics indicate:

Table 12

Crude male-labour productivity in UK metal mining

(tons metal-in-ores per man year)

| | Lead | Tin[4] |
|---|---|---|
| 1851 | 3.26 | 0.48 |
| 1861 | 3.54 | 0.52 |
| 1871 | 4.74 | 1.03 |
| 1881 | 4.41 | 0.82 |
| 1891 | 5.63 | 0.97 |
| 1901 | 4.58 | 0.69 |
| 1911 | 6.06 | 0.68 |

The upward trend in lead mining productivity is fairly clear. In the case of tin production, the pattern is masked by wide fluctuations but nevertheless a case can be made for overall gains compared with the 1850s and 1860s levels.

1 Cited in Burt, *Cornish mining*, p. 187.

2 Barton, *Tin mining*, pp. 192-3.

3 *Sessional Papers, House of Commons* (Cd.7) 1890-91, LXXVIII, 1: Metalliferous mines (Devon and Cornwall), Return of machinery and miners, pp. 2-3.

4 Calculated from census returns of employment, as in table 6, and published figures of ores mined (represented by metal content).

Throughout this study an implicit theme has been the relationship between technological factors and capital formation, for example in the analysis of depreciation rates and the retirement of assets. There are a number of issues which could be raised to further this kind of study but would first require much basic research aimed at providing more data on levels of investment, life of plant and the cost of alternative types of technology within the industry over time. One such problem is raised by H J Habakkuk when he suggests that American entrepreneurs in the nineteenth century employed technology of less life-span than that in Britain, in order to maximise returns from a capital-intensive form of production. American machinery, being retired after a shorter working life, enabled the capitalisation of rapid rates of technological progress.[1] This idea could be examined with an analysis of differential rates of depreciation, the cost of labour and other factors.

In broad terms, a model of the changing capital requirements of an individual mine could be generated. This would require an examination of the investment in and technological requirements of a mine at a number of distinct stages in the opening up of a mineral deposit. These stages would include early development and location of the ore bodies, a period of high circulating capital requirements and no output, a stage of rapid expansion of ore reserves with high fixed capital requirements and low output, a period of maturity with stable fixed and circulating capital requirements, and a period of decline, particularly relevant in the case of late nineteenth-century south-west mining, when output falls. Do entrepreneurs then involve themselves in heavy capital expenditure in order to counteract declining market prices and falling ore-grades or do they run down expenditure in anticipation of eventual closure? These kinds of questions could be attempted, given more data.

One theme that is clear to emerge in such a survey is that of the options open to Cornish mine owners in the prevailing market conditions after the 1860s. Considering the factors of production, land was strictly limited; lateral extension of ore deposits was rare after the mid-nineteenth century. Labour was becoming increasingly scarce after the mass emigrations in the post copper-collapse years of the late 1860s and the 1870s.[2] In these conditions more capital-intensive forms of production, allied with mining in depth, were the only options left to the survivors of each collapse in metal prices.

Study of capital formation in mining is essential to a full understanding of the economics of the industry and, as recently suggested by an American writer, to a full appreciation of the implications of resource depletion and the strategies open for their conservation.[3] In this practical context, study of past trends in capital formation and technological change in the mining industries must be pursued.

1 *American and British technology*, pp. 54-5.

2 It is estimated that in one year, 1868, over 8000 miners emigrated. Over the 1870s as a whole the population of Cornwall fell drastically. See Barton, *Tin mining*, p. 134, and Hamilton-Jenkin, *The Cornish miner*, pp. 321-40.

3 Orris C Herfindahl, *Copper costs and prices 1870-1957* (Baltimore: Johns Hopkins Press, 1959) pp. 5-6.

# A NOTE ON HOUSEBUILDING IN EXETER 1867-1940

Brian Clapp

How did housebuilding in Exeter between 1867 and 1940 compare with national trends? If data existed only for the ancient city of Exeter on its constricted site, a comparison would have little meaning. Fortunately the material available for Exeter includes that relating to the extensive suburbs of Heavitree and St Thomas that were absorbed by the city before the first world war. Between 1919 and 1939 further boundary extensions, mostly into open country, doubled the city's acreage without at the time greatly increasing its population. Until the present day there has never been a time, therefore, in the past hundred years when Exeter builders have been without land to develop, a situation which contrasts sharply with the position of many English cities, so that a comparison between Exeter and national trends is not without interest.

But there is difficulty in discussing housebuilding in Exeter between 1867 and 1919 because the only data that is available relates to house plans deposited by builders, not to houses actually built. The number of house plans has to be compared with Weber's well-known estimates of the number of houses built in Great Britain.[1] The question arises: How are we to compare the number of houses built with plans proposed? Luckily, for Exeter, from 1920 to 1950 we have information both on plans and on houses actually built. From this evidence it can be seen, as one would expect, that builders submitted more plans than they felt able to turn into houses but that most of the plans did materialise, usually with no more than a brief time lag.

As table 1 shows, rather more than two-thirds of the plans deposited were carried into effect. Further analysis shows that a time lag of one year between plan and completion gives the best fit, though admittedly the fit is not much better than if a two-year lag or no lag at all is assumed. Also, the number of plans deposited fluctuates much more sharply than the number of completions. In their most optimistic moods - in 1928 and 1934 - builders deposited plans nearly twice as fast as they were building houses. In years of uncertainty and contraction - 1939 and 1940, for example - the flow of plans dried up more quickly than the actual work of construction.

If the same relationship held good for earlier periods it is not unreasonable to set Exeter plans against British completions for the years 1867-1919. The Exeter figures will clearly be more volatile but they should reflect faithfully enough the underlying trend of housebuilding in the city and its suburbs.

1 Printed in John Parry Lewis, *Building cycles and Britain's economic growth* (Macmillan, 1965) Appendix 4, 'Indices of housebuilding 1851-1913', pp. 301-19. There are official statistics of housebuilding only for 1924 and succeeding years.

Table 1

Plans deposited and houses built in Exeter, 1920-1950*

| | Plans | Completions | | Plans | Completions |
|---|---|---|---|---|---|
| 1920 | 22 | - | 1936 | 552 | 362 |
| 1921 | 29 | 9 | 1937 | 384 | 322 |
| 1922 | 59 | 30 | 1938 | 365 | 345 |
| 1923 | 149 | 39 | 1939 | 157 | 266 |
| 1924 | 144 | 84 | 1940 | 9 | 62 |
| 1925 | 274 | 161 | 1941 | - | - |
| 1926 | 366 | 262 | 1942 | - | - |
| 1927 | 339 | 259 | 1943 | - | - |
| 1928 | 482 | 279 | 1944 | 3 | - |
| 1929 | 326 | 236 | 1945 | 103 | - |
| 1930 | 400 | 249 | 1946 | 193 | 46 |
| 1931 | 426 | 264 | 1947 | 118 | 92 |
| 1932 | 368 | 269 | 1948 | 122 | 53 |
| 1933 | 335 | 340 | 1949 | 214 | 97 |
| 1934 | 682 | 344 | 1950 | 117 | 85 |
| 1935 | 471 | 275 | Total | 7209 | 4830 |

* Council houses are not included in this table. The City built 2256 houses between 1919 and 1939. The corresponding figures for 1946-50 are unsatisfactory because they include pre-fabricated houses and war damaged houses restored by the City. The Exeter data on plans deposited and houses completed 1867-1950 were collected by the late Bernard Weber in 1952-3. The raw data are now in the possession of Professor John Parry Lewis, who has kindly made it available to the writer of this note.

At least until the end of the nineteenth century, as table 2 shows, Exeter builders went their own way without too much regard for national trends. The national building boom that led to nearly half a million houses being constructed in 1875-8 is not reflected in the Exeter figures. Not until 1877 are large numbers of plans deposited, with substantial numbers, too, in 1878 and 1879. The 1880s and early 1890s was a flat period nationally for housebuilding but for Exeter builders the 1880s began with a burst of optimism which was sustained (after a pause in 1881-4) to the very end. Then there is a sharp drop in Exeter deposits in 1890 and 1891. But recovery came earlier in Exeter than in the country as a whole, the number of plans deposited in Exeter trebling between 1891 and 1892. Four years later, a national building boom began. In 1896 over 100,000 houses were built in a year for the first time since 1878. Output remained at a higher level until 1907 after which there was a rapid descent to low levels of output. By

Table 2

Housebuilding in Britain and Exeter 1867-1914

| | GB houses (000) | Exeter plans | | GB houses (000) | Exeter plans | | GB houses (000) | Exeter plans |
|---|---|---|---|---|---|---|---|---|
| 1867 | 65 | 102 | 1883 | 82 | 72 | 1899 | 156 | 69 |
| 1868 | 70 | 41 | 1884 | 82 | 175 | 1900 | 140 | 211 |
| 1869 | 77 | 100 | 1885 | 77 | 151 | 1901 | 140 | 182 |
| 1870 | 86 | 79 | 1886 | 75 | 216 | 1902 | 154 | 270 |
| 1871 | 90 | 46+ | 1887 | 79 | 137 | 1903 | 157 | 288 |
| 1872 | 94 | 42 | 1888 | 80 | 210 | 1904 | 137 | 211 |
| 1873 | 82 | 51 | 1889 | 80 | 207 | 1905 | 127 | 560 |
| 1874 | 91 | 50 | 1890 | 76 | 48 | 1906 | 131 | 449 |
| 1875 | 120 | 25 | 1891 | 79 | 34 | 1907 | 121 | 421 |
| 1876 | 131 | 65 | 1892 | 84 | 100 | 1908 | 101 | 219 |
| 1877 | 124 | 153 | 1893 | 86 | 102 | 1909 | 99 | 95 |
| 1878 | 106 | 85 | 1894 | 91 | 90 | 1910 | 86 | 36 |
| 1879 | 86 | 92 | 1895 | 90 | 127 | 1911 | 68 | 66 |
| 1880 | 83 | 198 | 1896 | 107 | 145 | 1912 | 53 | 46 |
| 1881 | 79 | 83 | 1897 | 130 | 126 | 1913 | 54 | 44 |
| 1882 | 82 | 47 | 1898 | 158 | 82 | 1914 | 48 | 91 |

Source: Weber's data reprinted in Brian R Mitchell and Phyllis Deane, *Abstract of British historical statistics* (Cambridge UP, 1962) p. 239.

+ According to the 1871 census 61 houses were under construction in Exeter in 1871.

1912 fewer houses were being built that at any time in the previous fifty years. This particular cycle is closely mirrored in the Exeter series. Large numbers of plans were deposited in 1895-7 matching the rise in national activity that became marked in 1896. After a pause in 1898-9, Exeter builders deposited plans at an astonishing rate during the years 1900-8. In 1908 248 houses were built in the city, about 0.2 per cent of the national output.[1] Then there was a relapse. In the years before the outbreak of the war Exeter's builders were putting in no more plans than they had deposited in the depressed early 1870s. The comparisons possible between Exeter and the national scene are summarised in index form in table 3.

1 Robert Newton, *Victorian Exeter* (Leicester UP, 1968) p. 304.

Table 3

An index of housebuilding 1867-1914

| | 1867-76 | 1877-86 | 1887-96 | 1897-1906 | 1907-14 |
|---|---|---|---|---|---|
| Great Britain (houses) | 100 | 97 | 94 | 158 | 87 |
| Exeter (plans) | 100 | 211 | 199 | 407 | 212 |

Almost all the new houses in Exeter during this period were erected by private builders. By 1914 the City Council had built only 49 houses, a tiny contribution to Exeter's stock of buildings.

During the inter-war years, as table 4 demonstrates, Exeter followed national trends much more closely. The 1914-18 war had completely disrupted housebuilding - only 4 plans were deposited in 1915, 2 in 1916 and none in 1917 and 1918. It was not until 1921 that any privately-owned houses were completed in Exeter. In the following two years the number of houses built remained small, the expansion of housebuilding in Exeter lagging behind the general trend. Nationally a modest number of houses was completed in 1923 and by 1924 output was approaching its highest pre-war level. But it was not until 1926 that the average level of the 1900s was exceeded and more than 200 houses were completed in a year in Exeter. For the rest of the inter-war period Exeter builders were extraordinarily busy, producing year-by-year rather more than 0.1 per cent of the country's new houses.[1] But by contrast with the period before 1914, the City Council was much more active, building houses at just under one-third of the rate of private builders.

But this activity does not all represent a net addition to the housing stock of Exeter. The survival until 1942 of the picturesque and ancient Exeter High Street shows that in a small provincial city the demands of commerce could be met without substantial redevelopment. Nor did railway-building result in much destruction of property. Some demolition there undoubtedly was but not on the scale that characterised the redevelopment of the City of London and great provincial cities like Manchester and Leeds. Between the wars, however, the City Council cleared a great deal of slum property, especially in the West Quarter of Exeter, and it is likely that municipal action was responsible for the destruction of more old property than privately-owned businesses and railway companies. Even so, the rate of demolition lagged far behind the rate of building, so that the housing stock grew and grew faster than the population. In 1861, for example, the census enumerated 34,000 people living in 5400 houses; in 1901 46,000 people

1 But as noted above, p. 57, only half the 1908 proportion of 0.2 per cent.

Table 4

Housebuilding 1920-40

| | Great Britain (000) | Exeter | | Great Britain (000) | Exeter |
|---|---|---|---|---|---|
| 1920 | 30 | - | 1931 | 210 | 264 |
| 1921 | 76 | 9 | 1932 | 218 | 269 |
| 1922 | 85 | 30 | 1933 | 275 | 340 |
| 1923 | 66 | 39 | 1934 | 336 | 344 |
| 1924 | 131 | 84 | 1935 | 351 | 275 |
| 1925 | 174 | 161 | 1936 | 265 | 362 |
| 1926 | 222 | 262 | 1937 | 362 | 322 |
| 1927 | 255 | 259 | 1938 | 359 | 345 |
| 1928 | 207 | 279 | 1939 | 256 | 266 |
| 1929 | 212 | 236 | 1940 | 95 | 62 |
| 1930 | 202 | 249 | | | |

Source: Great Britain: Mitchell and Deane, *Historical statistics*, p. 239.
Exeter: Bernard Weber data.

Table 5 provides a comparison in index form based on the information set out in Tables 1 and 4 between the course of events in Exeter and in Great Britain in the 1920s and 1930s.

Table 5

An index of housebuilding 1920-39

| | Great Britain | Exeter | |
|---|---|---|---|
| | houses | houses | plans |
| 1920-9 | 100 | 100 | 100 |
| 1930-9 | 201 | 224 | 189 |

were living in 9400 houses and in 1951 76,000 people were living in 20,000 'structurally separate dwellings occupied'. There was a steady fall in the number of persons per house, as table 6 shows.

Table 6

Number of persons per house 1861-1951

| 1861 | 1871 | 1881 | 1891 | 1901 | 1911 | 1921 | 1931 | 1951 |
|---|---|---|---|---|---|---|---|---|
| 6.3 | 5.9 | 5.7 | 5.4 | 5.0 | 4.7 | 4.5 | 4.3 | 3.8 |

Source: *UK Census of Population* (HMSO)

These apparently comforting figures are not conclusive evidence of improved housing conditions. If the whole population had lived in houses as the word is commonly understood and those houses had been of a standard and unchanging size, table 6 would indeed chronicle a substantial improvement. Unfortunately a house might be one large room in a big old house let in flats or two rooms over a shop or a four-roomed cottage or a large block of flats. What is worse, a block of flats might be recorded as one house at one census and two dozen 'houses' at the next. In order to overcome these problems of definition, the census began in 1891 to enumerate the number of tenements and, in particular, to record the number of inhabitants of each tenement with fewer than five rooms. In 1891 and 1901, however, there was confusion in the minds of enumerators about the definition of a tenement and of a room. Some enumerators counted sculleries, lobbies, even landings, as rooms, with the result that the early data on overcrowding have to be treated with reserve. For what they are worth, the figures appear to show that the level of overcrowding in Exeter declined, most markedly in the 1890s and from 1931.

Table 7

Population in Exeter living in overcrowded conditions 1891-1951

| | 1891 | 1901 | 1911 | 1921 | 1931 | 1951 |
|---|---|---|---|---|---|---|
| More than two per room (per cent) | 7.1+ | 4.8+ | 4.4 | 4.9 | 3.7 | 0.2 |
| More than one per room (per cent) | 21.3+ | 17.8+ | 36.1 | - | 30.7 | 4.2 |

+ These figures refer to tenements of one to four rooms; the figures for 1911 and after refer to all tenements.

Source: *UK Census of Population*

Since there was relatively little demolition of property in the older parts of the city until slum clearance began between the wars, new housing tended to be built on the outskirts of Exeter and of its suburbs - Heavitree, St Thomas and Countess Wear. By the 1860s a continuous line of ribbon development already linked Exeter and Heavitree along the Heavitree Road and (not quite so thoroughly) along Magdalen Road. Holloway Street, on the road to Countess Wear and Topsham, was lined with houses but, apart from a few large properties like Coaver and Bellair, the Topsham Road ran through open country. To the north-east development had scarcely got beyond the eastern end of Sidwell Street and to the north along Longbrook Street and Pennsylvania Road few houses were to be seen beyond the railway line. By 1890 the edge of the city had moved further out. Polsloe Road and Union Road now marked the limits to the east and north. Not a great deal of building had taken place in St Leonards: College Road and Raleigh Road had been laid out but the development of the lower end of St Leonard's Road, the Grove estate and the Roberts Road area was the work of the 1880s and 1890s. Barnardo Road on the site of the Baring's old house, Mount Radford, was developed after 1900. In the building boom of the late 1890s and early 1900s large tracts of land in the Mount Pleasant area and along the Pinhoe Road were developed. Much building in St Thomas dates from this period - the streets off Buller Road for example. There was also infilling much nearer the city centre - in Kimberley Road behind Holloway Street, for instance. To the north of the city, Velwell Road, Danes Road and Hoopern Street date from the depressed years for the building industry immediately before the first world war.

Between the wars large numbers of houses were built north of Union Road in Pennsylvania, to the east of the city along East Wonford Hill and the Honiton Road, towards Pinhoe along the Whipton Road, along the Topsham Road and in Countess Wear. Ribbon development was allowed along the Exeter by-pass, which skirted the eastern edge of the city. Some development took place to the north-west along and off the road to Cowley but the favoured areas for housebuilding have always been to the east, west and south of the city and to this day Exeter presents a slightly odd appearance on the map: to the north-west in Exwick open country is less than a mile from the Guildhall, to the east it is possible to travel twice as far before open country is reached and to the south-east there is only half a mile of open country between Exeter and Topsham four miles down the river.